THE SPIRITUAL WAY
MANUAL

BY
MOTHER BOLTON
RELIGIOUS OF THE CENACLE
ASSOCIATE PROFESSOR, DEPARTMENT OF EDUCATION
FOR THE TEACHING OF CHRISTIAN DOCTRINE
FORDHAM UNIVERSITY
NEW YORK CITY

2020
St. Augustine Academy Press
Homer Glen, Illinois

This book was originally published in 1930 by World Book Company.

This facsimile edition reprinted in 2020 by St. Augustine Academy Press.

Nihil Obstat

REV. ARTHUR J. SCANLAN, S.T.D.
Censor Librorum

Imprimatur

✠ PATRICK CARDINAL HAYES
Archbishop of New York

NEW YORK
December 8, 1929

ISBN: 978-1-64051-110-1

DI SUA SANTITA

DAL VATICANO, le 21 Février 1930

*To the honored Mother Superior General
of the Religious of the Cenacle*

The Holy Father accepts with great pleasure the set of four volumes of The Spiritual Way written by one of your religious to facilitate the teaching of the Catechism in America. His Holiness thanks you with all his heart for this token of whole-hearted veneration and devotion to his august person and expresses his congratulations and fatherly interest in the work.

Happy to see the good results of this method of teaching the Catechism in the schools of the United States and rejoicing in the belief that these results will be multiplied elsewhere, His Holiness with all his heart gives, as a mark of his paternal affection and as a guarantee of the best of heavenly blessings upon this work, his special Apostolic Benediction.

E. Card. Pacelli

Secretary of State to His Holiness Pius XI

TRANSLATED FROM THE ORIGINAL IN FRENCH

As this Manual goes forth to teachers of Christian Doctrine, a work that has been done most lovingly is placed in their hands with a prayer that they may find joy in using it to plant seeds in children's souls which will develop and form spiritual men and women, who will be instruments in diffusing God's Light and Goodness wherever they may be.

May the Holy Spirit speak through every page of The Spiritual Way books, enlightening minds with His gifts of Wisdom, Understanding, Counsel, and Knowledge, and strengthening wills with His gifts of Fortitude, Piety, and Fear of the Lord.

And may all teachers and children who use these books listen to the Voice of the Holy Spirit and thus from day to day become better acquainted with this Divine Teacher; for Jesus has said, " The Paraclete, the Holy Ghost, whom the Father will send in my name, he will teach you all things, and bring all things to your mind, whatsoever I shall have said to you." (St. John 14 : 26).

THE AUTHOR

Contents

	PAGE
BASIC PRINCIPLES	1
A FUNDAMENTAL SPIRITUAL PRINCIPLE	1
OBJECTIVES IN TEACHING CHRISTIAN DOCTRINE	2
WHAT IS THE CATECHISM?	3
THE SPIRITUAL WAY SERIES	4
RESULTS OF EXPERIMENTATION	6
SELF-ACTIVITY	7
APPERCEPTION	9
INTEREST	12
BIBLE STUDY	14
VITALIZING SCRIPTURE VERSES THROUGH MUSIC	16
ORGANIZATION AND ARRANGEMENT OF SUBJECT MATTER	19
SOURCE MATERIAL FOR THE SERIES	27
BOOK ONE	27
Topic One: God the Creator	27
Topic Two: God Our Loving Father	29
Topic Three: The One Whose Power Can Protect All People	32
Topic Four: The One Whose Light Can Solve the Problems of All People	33
BOOK TWO	34
Topic Five: God's Image and Likeness in Us	34
Topic Six: Why God Made Us to His Image and Likeness	38
Topic Seven: The Kingdom of Noblest Princes and Princesses	40
Topic Eight: The Failure of the First Noble Prince and Princess	47
Topic Nine: Untrue Princes and Princesses	50

Contents

	PAGE
BOOK THREE	52
Topic Ten: The Blessed Trinity	52
Topic Eleven: Jesus, God and Man	54
Topic Twelve: Mary, Mother of Jesus	56
Topic Thirteen: The Sacrifices of the Old Law	57
Topic Fourteen: The Holy Sacrifice of the Mass	58
BOOK FOUR	62
Topic Fifteen: Jesus' Church	62
Topic Sixteen: The Coming of the Light of Grace	64
Topic Seventeen: The Font of Mercy	65
Topic Eighteen: The Living Bread	68
Topic Nineteen: Living in the King's Service	70
Topic Twenty: Strength for the King's Service	71
THE INTERPRETATION OF THE PICTURES	75
PROJECTS	90
ADDITIONAL TESTS AND PROBLEMS	100
ANSWERS TO THE TESTS	114
THE DOCTRINAL POINTS OF THE BALTIMORE CATECHISM IN THE SPIRITUAL WAY	161

BASIC PRINCIPLES

A FUNDAMENTAL SPIRITUAL PRINCIPLE

It is the teaching of Catholic theology that God Himself dwells within the soul where the Light of Grace is shining, and that He is always striving to pour into that soul an ever-increasing measure of Divine Life, to make the mind and will in which He dwells more perfectly conformed to His Own image and likeness.

Next to the priest who can administer the Sacraments, those who teach Christian Doctrine, whether in the home or in the school, have the most sacred position with regard to the human soul. For the teacher of Christian Doctrine is an agent in helping to form the mind and the will of the child to the image and likeness of God. And such a work is holy because it is a participation in the work of God Himself.

The Church has always expected those who have the privilege of enlightening the minds of her children with the bright light of her doctrine to be themselves imbued with the reality of the doctrine of the indwelling of the Holy Ghost. Thus imbued, they will realize the Presence of that same Holy Spirit in children's souls, and work in conjunction with Him to fulfill His designs, instead of superimposing their own ideas on the child mind. Likewise, they will not allow the child to carry out any ideas of his own that are contrary to the voice of conscience, which is the direction of the Holy Spirit.

For the realization of the Presence of the Holy Spirit and the right of the individual soul to develop spiritually in accordance with God's designs upon it makes the teacher understand that his mission is to be an exterior aid to the Holy Spirit working in the interior of the soul.

With this realization teachers, supervisors, and all in authority over children, appreciating the privilege and responsibility which are theirs, feel the necessity of putting much time and patience into the practice of the art of teaching.

And in the light of the doctrine of the indwelling of the Blessed Trinity in souls in the state of grace, the Church has always been concerned less with the quantity of information imparted than with the patient, slow training which allows for the child's reactions and makes for substantial spiritual growth.

OBJECTIVES IN TEACHING CHRISTIAN DOCTRINE

If the religious education of a normal child does not result in such an understanding and love of Christian Doctrine truths that they become living principles in the child's life, this is a disaster in the Mystical Body of Christ.

Ask yourself these questions:

Is everyone or no one responsible for the disaster?

Does the mere memorizing of a Catechism statement mean that the child has an intelligent understanding of it, or that he has acquired the power to apply this principle to the problems of his life?

When our children leave the elementary school, should our teaching have imbued them with a satisfied attitude of mind that their religious studies are finished, or with an active interest in Christian Doctrine and a desire to read and study more?

Is your first objective, as a teacher of Christian Doctrine, to help children to memorize a required number of Catechism statements? Or is your first objective to lay a firm foundation for future doctrinal teaching and spiritual growth by developing in the child mind a knowledge of God as Creator and Loving Father, and in his will a desire to love and obey?

Which method will lead to the highest and truest spiritual activity in the life of the child — the method in which the teacher gives a number of facts in a short space of time, telling the child how he must act in the light of this knowledge; or the method in which the teacher presents the facts slowly and in such a manner as to give the child mind the opportunity to assimilate them and, after they are assimilated, to apply the facts to his own life?

Which will give the greater motive force toward the leading of a truly Catholic life — a course of study built upon the basic principle of the mastery of a Christian Doctrine text; or a course which has for its basic principle the development of the mind and the will of the child so that his life will reflect the Christian Doctrine text?

WHAT IS THE CATECHISM?

The Catechism is a compendium of theological truths in a condensed form. It gives only the text of the lesson. The lesson itself should be carefully planned and logically developed. For if the lesson is not well developed, there will be no assimilation; and without assimilation there can be no spiritual growth or spiritual strength for the child.

All discussions on doctrinal matters which have arisen in the history of the Church have centered around doctrinal topics.

In the Councils of the Church every point that had a definite bearing on a particular topic was discussed, conclusions were reached, and the Catechism statement was evolved. This was a reasonable development.

In much the same way that the Catechism statements have evolved historically, they must also evolve in the individual mind.

Children must think about and discuss doctrinal points before the Catechism statement will be an active principle in their lives.

THE SPIRITUAL WAY SERIES

The Spiritual Way is a series of books which build a solid structure of Christian Doctrine, using the Catechism as the basis and developing inductively a mastery of the doctrinal truths prescribed by the Church. The series includes Books One, Two, Three, and Four. In these four books the teaching centers around twenty main doctrinal Topics, by means of which the fundamental doctrines of Holy Church are presented slowly and with scientific care.

At the end of the discussion of each doctrinal point, the Catechism statement is given.

The books contain all the accessory materials required to teach the matter effectively. In accordance with the best practices in progressive teaching, the child is given an opportunity for various forms of expression through tests, problems, and projects.

This series is designed to teach children first *to think* dogma,

Basic Principles

then *to express* dogma, and through understanding and love *to practice* it in their daily lives.

The Spiritual Way leads the child along a new path in spiritual growth. It contributes new impetus and new desires to continue progress in the spiritual life, and it helps to establish right habits of spiritual behavior.

The series constitutes a logical course in Christian Doctrine, giving a clear and simple presentation of the fundamental doctrines of the Faith.

Book One has been designed for children who are beginning this logical course at the age of about eight years. But as Book One lays the foundation for a solid course of instruction, whatever the age of the person to be instructed, this book should be taught first and the others should follow in consecutive order. The difficult doctrine of Book One is presented in language which a child of eight can readily grasp. To insure this, the choice of words has been standardized according to the frequency list of Thorndike's *Teachers' Word Book*, which proved serviceable because many Bible and doctrinal words were included in the author's vocabulary research.

As children go on using *The Spiritual Way* from year to year, they become able to assimilate more and more points of doctrine. So the books become gradually larger, until by the time Book Four is finished the content of the Catechism is not only covered but developed and given a practical value in the life of the child through various forms of application. The language also becomes more mature as the series progresses.

Book One contains four Topics; Book Two, five Topics; Book Three, five Topics; Book Four, six Topics.

This series is unified in its plan of development; hence, for effective teaching, the teacher should become familiar with the Topics preceding the one being used. This means, for example, that the teacher using Book Four should be very familiar with the contents of the three preceding books.

It is the purpose of *The Spiritual Way* to lead the child to think. Mental alertness is stimulated and encouraged. The achievement standards that are frequently used place a premium on the attention of those who master the matter and mark with definite rating those who have been mentally inert.

RESULTS OF EXPERIMENTATION

The Spiritual Way is the result of years of experimentation in the field of Christian Doctrine. The lessons were used in manuscript form with many classes of children and later as the basis of courses given to both religious and secular teachers of Christian Doctrine.

The interest thus aroused and the results produced brought requests for publication in book form so that the lessons could be available for use in schools and catechetical centers.

The first publication entitled *The Spiritual Way* presented a series of lessons for the use of the teacher and in this form has gone through several editions.

The success of these books, the results obtained, and the fact that the lessons have produced in children a real interest in Christian Doctrine have brought about the present rewriting in enlarged and perfected form. So the teacher receiving this series of books can feel assured that their worth has been proved by their use in many places, by many teachers, over a long period of time.

SELF-ACTIVITY

Educators have endeavored through their study of child psychology to determine the principles which, when applied in teaching, will lead to the fullest development of the faculties of the soul.

The results of their labors have been both enlightening and helpful. And we find these fundamental principles underlying all good teaching from that of the Master Teacher in the pages of the Gospel to the schoolroom of today.

One fundamental principle applied throughout the Gospels is that which calls for coöperation on the part of the one learning. The parable of the talents told in the Gospel of St. Matthew 25 : 15–30 is a good illustration of both the application and the teaching of this principle.

In the language of modern educators, the Master expected His servant to apply the principle of self-activity and to use the one talent He had given him in order to attain his fullest spiritual development. And the use of the parable of the talents was the Master Teacher's way of teaching us this principle.

St. Ignatius in his famous book, *The Spiritual Exercises*, makes a comparison between physical activities such as walking and all bodily exercises, and spiritual activities such as prayer, meditation, self-examination, and other exercises of the mind and will. He says that " the name of spiritual exercises is applied to any method of preparing and disposing the soul to free itself from all inordinate affections, and after it has freed itself from them, to seek and find the will of God concerning the ordering of life for the salvation of one's soul."

St. Ignatius here formulates the principle of *spiritual self-activity*.

The Spiritual Way endeavors to develop in the child full spiritual self-activity, which will bring progressive spiritual growth, always keeping a true perspective with regard to the rights of God and of properly constituted authority. St. Ignatius says, " It is not to know much but it is to understand and savour the matter interiorly that fills and satisfies the soul." To grow thus spiritually, the child must be given a medium for spiritual self-activity. In *The Spiritual Way* the theological facts as given in condensed form in the Catechism are developed in the child mind by means of logical questions, problems taken from the child's daily experience, projects which apply the doctrinal message to the child's life, and tests which stimulate spiritual activity.

True spiritual activity in its various forms must be nourished by grace. In the words of *The Imitation of Christ:*

> Thy grace is the mistress of truth, the teacher of discipline, the light of the heart, the consoler of anguish, the banisher of sorrow, the expeller of fear, the nurse of devotion, the producer of tears. . . . Therefore, O Lord, let Thy grace always go before and follow after me, and make me ever intent upon good works, through Jesus Christ Thy Son. (Book III, Chapter LV)

The salvation of souls is an individual matter; and so the child should be trained to express, under safe guidance, the activity to which a growth in grace urges him. The Church exists for the salvation of souls, and the dogmas of the Church are helps to this main purpose. Hence the very best possible means should be used in order that the dogmas of the Church may serve the purpose for which the Church exists.

APPERCEPTION

Jesus, the Model Teacher of Christian Doctrine, during His three years of public teaching constantly applied the principle of teaching unknown facts through the medium of what is already known. Thus He applied the principle known to educators as *apperception*.

When Jesus wanted to explain His Own poverty, he used as an apperceptive basis the familiar truth that " the foxes have holes and the birds of the air nests; but the Son of man hath not where to lay his head." (St. Luke 9: 58)

When Jesus wished to teach absolute confidence in God, He called the attention of those to whom He was speaking to the protection given to the birds. He said, " They neither sow, nor do they reap, nor gather into barns: and your heavenly Father feedeth them. Are not you of much more value than they?" And throughout the rest of the sixth chapter of St. Matthew the Master Teacher leads those who listen to Him to confidence by directing them to observe God's tender care for creatures with which they are familiar.

When the proper direction of self-activity has been secured by utilizing facts already known, the mind of the child must then be given an impetus which will create a desire to receive the new knowledge. This impetus, frequently called the *aim*, may be given in the form of a challenging question or statement, a problem, or a project. In whatever form it is given, its purpose is to motivate the lesson by arousing the child's curiosity and causing him to desire the new knowledge.

We find numerous illustrations of motivation in the lessons left us in the Gospels. For instance, when Jesus was about to present the doctrine of His Divinity to His Apostles in a formal way, instead of telling them the fact as a direct statement, He first prepared their minds by asking this question: " Whom do men say that the Son of man is? " (St. Matthew 16:13) And when they had answered, He gave further motivation with the challenging question: " But whom do you say that I am? "

In this way He drew from Peter the truth, " Christ is the Son of the living God," which He wished to teach.

Then Jesus, the Model Teacher, confirmed the answer given by His Apostle in these words: " Blessed art thou, Simon Bar-Jona: because flesh and blood hath not revealed it to thee, but my Father, who is in heaven."

Another excellent illustration of motivation is given in St. John 4:5–27, where Jesus teaches a twofold lesson — the doctrine of grace and the truth that He is the Messias.

Jesus talks to the Samaritan woman at Jacob's well and stimulates her curiosity by the request, " Give me to drink." Because of her historical background, she shows her interest and surprise by the answer, " How dost thou, being a Jew, ask of me to drink, who am a Samaritan woman? For the Jews do not communicate with the Samaritans."

With her curiosity thus aroused, Jesus proceeds to lead her on from natural water to a knowledge of sanctifying grace, " the living water." But knowledge of grace will not bring eternal life; so the stimulation of interest is carried on until desire for possession is reached. Then Jesus said, " He that shall drink of the water that I will give him, shall not thirst forever." And " the woman saith to Him: Sir, give me this water."

Thus far the lesson has been motivated and the motivation carried along by interest; but the main point of the lesson,

Basic Principles

which is that Jesus is the expected Messias, is still to be taught. So Jesus arouses her curiosity still more. He says to her, "Go, call thy husband," and then completely surprises her by revealing His knowledge of her past life. For in reply to her statement, "I have no husband," He says to her, "Thou hast said well, I have no husband. For thou hast had five husbands: and he whom thou now hast, is not thy husband."

Having thus convinced her that He is a prophet, He still leads her on very carefully until she says, "I know that the Messias cometh (who is called Christ); therefore, when he is come, he will tell us all things."

With her mind thus carefully and thoroughly prepared, He makes known the great truth He intended from the beginning to teach: "I am he (the Messias) who am speaking with thee."

Following the example of the Master Teacher, every good teacher endeavors to link new knowledge with that already familiar to each child and to motivate the lesson through the stimulation of the child's curiosity.

By studying the following portion of a lesson from Book One of *The Spiritual Way* series, the teacher can see how apperception and motivation have prepared the way for the presentation of new knowledge. The doctrinal point to be taught is that God is the Creator of heaven and earth and all things. The child's mental activity is stimulated by several suggestions and questions, giving him an urge to know if there is anyone who has the power to make things out of nothing. One of the suggestions is developed in the passage quoted on the following page.

Let us make believe that you are a carpenter.
Suppose you are going to make a box.
What things do you need to make a box?

> *Boards, nails, a hammer, and other things.*

Or perhaps you want to make a wagon.
What must you have to make the wagon?

> *Boards, nails, wheels, and other things.*

Now suppose someone asks you to make either a box or a wagon.
But you have no boards or nails.
What would you answer?

> *I cannot make either the box or the wagon unless I have the things I need to make it.*

The child is then challenged with several questions:

Suppose you had nothing at all, what could you make?

> *I could not make anything.*

So you see, *you* cannot make something out of nothing.
Do you know any boy or girl who can make things out of nothing?
Do you know any man or woman who can make things out of nothing?

But there is Someone Who has the power to make things out of nothing.

INTEREST

Unless motivation grows into an active, sustained interest, there can be no prolonged self-activity, for to create a desire to receive new knowledge is futile *if this desire is not maintained.*

Many educators tell us that there is no real learning without interest. But educators do not agree concerning the importance of the part which the principle of interest plays in the educational scheme.

There are two main points of view concerning interest.

One of these maintains that interest is a means toward the acquiring of knowledge in a pleasurable way. The other view is that interest itself is a better end than knowledge.

In accordance with this second view, the teacher who at the end of the course of instruction leaves the child with an abiding interest which creates an appetite for more and deeper knowledge of the subject is the greater teacher. In Christian Doctrine teaching, such a teacher has accomplished a great work in the spiritual life of the child.

The student is not always interested in the subject itself at the outset; but if the end for which the subject is being pursued can hold his interest and is kept in mind, the interest will be sustained until that end is secured. And the maintaining of interest in a worth-while end has very definite spiritual values.

One of its greatest spiritual values is that when the energy is strongly directed toward something good, the mind is not turned upon such things as have a deteriorating effect upon the morals of the individual.

Another spiritual value derived from the maintaining of interest in a worth-while end is will training. And the training of the will is one of the essential functions in Catholic education, for without activity of the will there can be no sin or no holiness.

Thus it is evident that the proper training of the will to act in accordance with known truth is of greater spiritual value than any actual knowledge of a doctrinal point. For example, it is far more important that a child's will be so trained to right action that he will not steal than that he be able to state with great fluency: " Thou shalt not steal."

The greatest field for the activity of the will in the lesson is in the application, when the child consciously applies the newly acquired knowledge to his daily conduct. So if children are to know how to apply the Christian Doctrine principles in later life, the teacher should help them to acquire this extremely difficult art at the same time that they are learning the Christian Doctrine principle.

If every point of doctrine is thus made vital in the child's life, this training in making correct applications of doctrinal principles will be the basis for the making of correct applications as the need arises all through life. When through careful direction a child feels that he has discovered a Christian Doctrine principle, it is a great thing in his life, but it must be applied when the opportunity presents itself if the child is to attain substantial spiritual growth.

A good teacher of Christian Doctrine will motivate the lesson and use in her teaching every possible device to sustain interest until the principle is mastered. But realizing that indoctrination is not enough, the teacher will carry the interest through a series of applications to the child's life.

BIBLE STUDY

In order to familiarize children with Holy Scripture and make them desire to read it, it is well to have them memorize selected Scripture verses bearing upon the doctrinal point being taught. Where memorizing supplants a development lesson, we cannot be sure that the child has grasped anything of the new knowledge we intend to present. But it is very important that our Catholic children be able to elucidate points of doctrine by means of appropriate Bible texts. It is also important that the child become familiar with the

Basic Principles 15

best thoughts of the inspired writers because then his memory will be stored with high and holy thoughts, which should color his entire life, brightening it and helping him to rise above any sordid environment in which he may find himself.

Throughout *The Spiritual Way* series the child is continually given Scriptural references to prove and to elucidate the doctrinal points and is required to memorize many of the Scripture verses. In Books Three and Four of the series the child is carefully trained to use The Bible intelligently. This will establish a habit which will be valuable to him when his school days are over.

Many purposeful activities built upon Bible work are furnished in *The Spiritual Way* in the form of Bible hunts, tests, and projects. It may be of interest to the teacher to note what some of the Doctors of the early Church have said about the value of knowing Scripture texts.

St. Augustine says, " To read the Holy Scriptures is to obtain no slight knowledge of divine beatitude. He who desires to be ever in the company of God ought to pray and read without ceasing, for when we pray, we speak to God, and when we read (the Scriptures) God speaks to us."

And St. Basil advises all to know the Psalms : " The Psalm serves as a commencement for beginners; it is the means of advancing for those who progress; it is the support of those who attain to perfection : it is the voice of the Church."

St. Jerome advised a young widow to read each day a certain fixed number of verses. " Pay God this tribute," he wrote to her, " and never retire to rest without having first filled the basket of your heart with this provision of sacred verses."

And in more recent times " one of the most important

efforts made by Pope Leo XIII during his long and glorious pontificate was to promote a greater love and esteem for the Holy Scriptures. So anxious was he that his advice should be laid to heart, that he granted to everyone who should spend a quarter of an hour in reading or meditating on the Holy Book, a special indulgence."

MONSIGNOR JOHN S. VAUGHAN

VITALIZING SCRIPTURE VERSES THROUGH MUSIC

Pope Pius X in his famous Motu Proprio issued on the Feast of the Immaculate Conception in 1903 gives very careful instruction on the value of sacred music in the spiritual upbuilding of the faithful. The following excerpt states what he considers a fundamental principle.

> Sacred music being a complementary part of the solemn liturgy participates in the general scope of the liturgy, which is the Glory of God and the sanctification and edification of the faithful. Since its principal office is to clothe with suitable melody the liturgical text proposed for the understanding of the faithful, its proper aim is to add greater efficacy to the text, in order that through it the faithful may be more easily moved to devotion and better disposed for the reception of the fruits of Grace belonging to the celebration of the most holy mysteries.

Archbishop Blenk of New Orleans in his pastoral letter on the Motu Proprio of Pope Pius X, dated November 22, 1907, says:

> Man's tendency is to drift toward mere naturalism; the Church proposes to lift him to supernaturalism, and for this purpose puts before him, vividly and realistically, the spirit of prayer as opposed to that of the world. . . . She feeds the mind of man with constant readings from

Basic Principles

Sacred Scripture, firing his imagination the while so that he may grasp her great lesson not only with the mind but with the heart. For this purpose she illustrates — one might almost say dramatizes — the sacred text: dramatizes it to the eye by her beautiful ceremonial, and to the ear by uttering the words of the text, not in the ordinary speaking voice, but in the more elevated and musical tones in which the poets and especially the prophets delivered, in days gone by, their inspired messages.

In accordance with the traditions of the Church, throughout *The Spiritual Way* Bible verses are set to sacred music to aid the children to become more familiar with the text itself and to inspire them with greater devotion.
Pope Pius X also says:

>   Special efforts are to be made to restore the use of the Gregorian Chant by the people, so that the faithful may again take a more active part in the ecclesiastical offices, as was the case in ancient times.

And Archbishop Blenk says:

>   St. Gregory, when organizing the liturgy, provided it with suitable music, which music has never been surpassed either in form or in the power of expressing and inspiring that devotion which the Church intends. . . . Gregorian music is indeed prayer and nothing but prayer. It clothes the sacred text with melodies of a religious gravity so striking, of a pathos so tender and at the same time of such supernatural peace and purity as to raise our minds from all thoughts of earth, calming and collecting the soul, and inoculating us, almost unconsciously to ourselves, with the desire and love of heavenly things.

It is very significant to notice that the Second Council of Baltimore in 1866 recommends very earnestly in these words the teaching of the Gregorian Chant in parochial schools: " We consider it very desirable that the elements of Gregorian Chant be taught and exercised in the parochial schools." (II Baltimore 338.)

The Spiritual Way: Manual

In compliance with the desires expressed by the Second Council of Baltimore and by the famous Motu Proprio of Pope Pius X, Gregorian Chant is presented to the children who study *The Spiritual Way*.

In Book One, Topic One, the children are introduced to Gregorian Chant and taught the First Tone. When they have completed the series, they should be thoroughly familiar with the eight tones of the Chant.

ORGANIZATION AND ARRANGEMENT OF SUBJECT MATTER

BOOK ONE

Topic One

The first Topic presented in *The Spiritual Way* is " God the Creator." This arrangement is in harmony with the organization of the Baltimore Catechism, which teaches "God is Creator" first. It is also in harmony with the plan of *The Spiritual Exercises of St. Ignatius*, which lays down as its foundation and first principle " Man was created to praise, reverence, and serve God our Lord, and by this means to save his soul; and the other things on the face of the earth were created for man's sake, and in order to aid him in the prosecution of the end for which he was created."

The Topic " God the Creator " cannot be taught fully without also teaching about creatures. In *The Spiritual Way* the child learns the meaning of the term " creatures " and then studies the chief creatures, men and angels.

Topic Two

As one of the objects of *The Spiritual Way* series is to develop the statements of the Catechism, the second Topic, " God Our Loving Father," lays the foundation for teaching the third statement of the Catechism, " Man is a creature composed of body and soul, and made to the image and likeness of God."

The presence of sanctifying grace in the soul is the theological basis upon which the Fatherhood of God is established.

For this reason it is necessary in Topic Two to establish ideas concerning grace and its effects which are somewhat within the comprehension of the child.

As sanctifying grace becomes effective through its influence upon the soul, the soul's powers of knowing and loving are presented before the idea of grace.

Topic Three

The Apostles' Creed is taught in Chapter One of the Catechism. In the first division of the Apostles' Creed there are three ideas of God to be developed. These are that God is Creator, God is Father, and God is Almighty. God the Creator is developed in Topic One, God Our Father in Topic Two, and God is Almighty in Topic Three of *The Spiritual Way*. After these three ideas have been developed, the logical application is the first three petitions of The Lord's Prayer, the meaning of which should be carefully taught even though the child may have repeated the Our Father from babyhood.

Topic Four

After teaching that God is Almighty, the next point of the Catechism is to teach that God sees and knows all things. In *The Spiritual Way* these statements of the Catechism are taught inductively through a series of stories under the heading "The One Whose Light Can Solve the Problems of All People."

With the development of the Catechism statements presented in BOOK ONE, a firm foundation of spiritual truth is established. Upon this foundation a solid structure consisting of the doctrinal points of the Catechism and their application to everyday life can be built. It has been found that with young children it is necessary to spend a good deal of time laying this foundation and that it is therefore better to present only a very few Catechism statements in this first year of the course.

BOOK TWO

Topic Five

In Topic Five we build upon the foundation already laid in Topic Two of BOOK ONE. There the children were prepared to learn about God's image and likeness in us. They are now ready for an understanding of the Catechism statement, " Man is made to the image and likeness of God." Through experimentation it has been found that this Catechism statement contains so much that we must give the child mind ample time for assimilation. Consequently, this statement comes in Topic Five rather than as a part of Topic Two.

In Topic Five the terms " mind " and " will " are introduced and the effects of grace are further developed. In preparation for what is to be taught in later Topics concerning the indwelling of the Holy Ghost, the application of Topic Five teaches that the body is the temple of the soul and that the soul should rule the body.

Topic Six

When the child has been taught the meaning of the Catechism statement, " Man is made to the image and likeness of God," it is logical to present the reason why God made man to His Own image and likeness. This is done in Topic Six, which also includes the answers to the two Catechism questions: " Why did God make you ? " and " What must we do to save our souls ? "

As an application of this Topic, a foundation is laid for an understanding of the doctrine of the indwelling of the Holy Ghost in souls in the state of grace.

Topic Seven

A study of the Catechism question, " Why did God make you ? " requires some explanation of heaven, for the term " heaven " is included in the answer. The Catechism does not give a statement as to the meaning of heaven until the thirty-third chapter.

In *The Spiritual Way*, however, in Topic Seven heaven is presented. This necessitates the teaching of hell and purgatory also. It is appropriate to give the doctrine of the Communion of Saints as an application of a lesson on heaven and purgatory. A careful discussion of the doctrine is given in the Topic, although it is not found in all the Catechisms for the lower grades. Guardian angels seem to fit quite naturally into this setting, so something about them is introduced here.

Again, to reach this happiness of heaven, it is necessary to obey God's Commandments. This is the reason why the Commandments of the Old Law are introduced as applications.

Topic Eight

Chapter Four of the Catechism treats of our first parents, their disobedience, their punishment, and the effect upon us — in other words, the doctrine of original sin. In Topic

Organization and Arrangement

Eight of *The Spiritual Way* original sin is presented. Its causes and effects are discussed.

Five Commandments of the Old Law have already been taught. A careful foundation must be laid before the sixth Commandment can be presented upon a supernatural basis. This is done in the application of Topic Eight in *The Spiritual Way*.

Topic Nine

Following the order of the Catechism, mortal and venial sin are presented for special consideration in Topic Nine after original sin has been taught in Topic Eight.

The meaning of sin and its causes and effects have been thoroughly discussed in Topic Seven, but the term " sin " is not mentioned until we are ready to present a formal discussion of sin and the kinds of sin.

The basic law concerning the relation between sin and suffering is taught — the personal effect of sin upon the mind and will of the sinner and the personal suffering which follows sin. The child now has the necessary background for the completion of the doctrine of purgatory, which was first presented in Topic Seven.

The formal discussion of sin is completed in Topic Nine, and it is fitting that the formal study of the Commandments should be finished in the same book in which the discussion on sin closes.

BOOK THREE

Topic Ten

Before the definition "God is a spirit infinitely perfect" can be taught, a comprehensive background of knowledge must be given to the child. This is done in BOOK ONE and BOOK TWO.

In order to help prepare a background for some understanding of spirits — God, angels, and human souls — the first idea given in Topic Ten is that a spirit is not material. Having taught what a spirit is not, we reach the idea of what a spirit is, through a knowledge of what it can do.

The child knows that he has a mind which gives him the power to know and a will which gives him the power to love. He also knows that the mind and the will are powers of the soul.

Proceeding then from the known to the unknown, the conclusion can be reached that all spirits have the powers of knowing and loving.

In *The Spiritual Way* an apperceptive basis of humility is laid by making the child realize the utter incapacity of the human mind to understand even natural mysteries. With this realization, he is ready to study the greatest of all mysteries, the mystery of the Blessed Trinity.

The doctrine of the indwelling of the Holy Ghost, which was introduced in Topic Six, is further elaborated in this Topic.

Topic Eleven

The discussion of sin would naturally be followed by ideas concerning the Redemption. The Redemption, however, cannot be rightly taught until after the Topic on the Blessed Trinity has been presented. For this reason the subject matter treating of the Redemption is placed as Topic Eleven under the heading " Jesus, God and Man."

As it is valuable for children to become thoroughly familiar with the source book of the mystery of the Redemption, they are carefully taught in this Topic how to use this source book, the New Testament. It is also logical to add ways in which the Church celebrates some of the mysteries connected with Jesus, God and Man. The meaning of certain feasts is therefore introduced here.

Topic Twelve

No Catholic teaching concerning Jesus, God and Man, would be complete without a Topic about Mary, Mother of Jesus. The Immaculate Conception is taught first because this is the fundamental doctrine concerning the Blessed Virgin Mary.

Topics Thirteen and Fourteen

The logical conclusion to a study of the Redemption is its perpetuation — the Holy Sacrifice of the Mass. So in Topic Thirteen, by teaching the Sacrifice of the Old Law, a proper background is prepared for an understanding of the Holy Sacrifice of the Mass, which is taught in Topic Fourteen.

BOOK FOUR

BOOK FOUR is essentially devoted to the teaching of the Sacraments. The Church is the channel through which the grace of the Sacraments reaches the individual soul, as well as the guide and teacher left by Jesus. So it is appropriate that BOOK FOUR should be devoted to the Church and the Sacraments and that a Topic concerning the Church should precede the Topics on the Sacraments. The Commandments of the Church are taught as an application of the lesson on the Church.

The Sacrament of Confirmation is placed last in *The Spiritual Way* because in connection with the study of this Sacrament there is a discussion of the virtues, gifts, and beatitudes which open to the child a pathway through which he may catch glimpses of the heights of the spiritual life.

All the material given in this Topic can be used in higher grades and in preparing any person, whether child or adult, for Confirmation.

SOURCE MATERIAL FOR THE SERIES
BOOK ONE

TOPIC ONE: GOD THE CREATOR

Suppose that you as a teacher of Christian Doctrine intend to teach the following statements of the Catechism:

" God made the world."

" God is the Creator of heaven and earth and of all things."

You would not begin by having the two statements memorized. You would have a plan which would stimulate the child's interest and cause activity of his mind and will.

Any wise teacher before beginning to formulate a plan will make sure, first of all, that he understands the meaning of the doctrinal statement in accord with the mind of the Church, even though the statement itself has been thoroughly familiar to him since childhood.

What is the difference in meaning between the first and the second statements of the Catechism?

The first statement reads: " God made the world."

Heaven and earth and all things, as ordinarily considered, means the world.

The second statement is, therefore, equivalent to " God is the Creator of the world."

It can be seen, then, that the difference in the interpretation of these two statements hinges on the meaning of *make* and *create*.

In making a plan to teach that God is the Creator, it is necessary to know the meaning of *creature*. In *The Spiritual Way* a creature is defined as " anything God has made." Some children may need the teacher's help to understand that although everything created is a creature of God, everything was not made directly by God. To illustrate: It was man who made the table out of wood. But carried back to its first beginnings, there was a definite act of creation before man could make the table.

Then with the meaning of the statements clearly in mind, the next step in planning the lesson is to select some activity familiar in the child's life which will serve as a stepping stone to the development of the idea that God is the only One Who can make things out of nothing.

In Topic One, page 1, this step is carefully developed.

After the child is convinced that no person can make things out of nothing, he is given a mental urge in the following statement: "But there is Someone Who has the power to make things out of nothing."

The next question which arises for the teacher in making a plan is: Which avenue of approach shall I take to reach the new knowledge — that based upon reasoning only, or that based upon revelation and faith? Either approach can be used with success.

But it is well for the teacher of Christian Doctrine to lay a solid foundation of faith by letting the child know from the outset that one source of knowledge of Christian truths is Divine revelation. Therefore in Topic One the method of presenting new knowledge is based upon revelation and faith.

No lesson is complete without an application, and the application can be very wide and varied. In Topic One four points of application are given:

1. Why all things belong to God.
2. Appropriate Bible verses.
3. The poem "All Things Bright and Beautiful."
4. Bible verses set to music.

When Topic One has been well taught, and the idea of God as Creator has been properly established, two important tasks have been accomplished. First, a foundation stone of humility has been laid in the child's mind; and second, an attitude of reverence for God has been established in the child's life.

TOPIC TWO: GOD OUR LOVING FATHER

The reason given in Topic One for calling God *Creator* is the fact that God made us out of nothing.

God is Our Loving Father as well as the Creator; and before beginning to plan a lesson entitled " God Our Loving Father," it is necessary to find out the theological basis for calling God *Father*. First of all, it is understood that *father* and *child* in the restricted meaning of these terms are used only when both are of the same nature. We know that our nature is human and God's nature is Divine. On this basis we must conclude that we have no right to call God our Father. What, then, is it that gives us the right to call God Father?

The Catechism teaches that we are made children of God at Baptism through sanctifying grace.

In the Baltimore Catechism the definition of sanctifying grace is: " By grace I mean a supernatural gift of God bestowed on us, through the merits of Jesus Christ, for our salvation."

There is nothing in this definition to make known to us why sanctifying grace makes us children of God.

In order to teach a lesson entitled " God Our Loving Father," it is necessary to establish the fact that we are sharers in something of God Himself.

St. Thomas tells us the greatness of the gift of grace in the following words: "The gift of grace surpasses every capability of created nature, since it is nothing short of a partaking of the Divine Nature, which exceeds every other nature."

St. Peter in his second epistle tells us that through the promises of Jesus we may become "partakers of the divine nature." (2 St. Peter 1:4)

And the definition of grace as given in the Catechism of the Council of Trent tells us that grace is a divine quality inherent in the soul. The following is a quotation from this Catechism.

> But grace, according to the definition of the Council of Trent, a definition to which, under pain of anathema we are bound to defer, not only remits sin but is also a divine quality inherent in the soul, and, as it were, a brilliant light that effaces all those sins which obscure the luster of the soul, and invests it with increased brightness and beauty.

This definition of grace shows that we are sharers in something of God Himself — God's Nature, God's Life, God's Light, God's Beauty.

The fact that through grace we are sharers in God's Nature and God's Life can be introduced a little later in the curriculum when the children are more mature.

In Topic Two God's Light and Beauty are used because, after a wide experience in using this idea of grace, it has been found that it brings a real spiritual awakening to the child.

The steps followed in presenting the idea of grace as a participation in God's Light and Beauty are

1. Through sunlight one can see natural beauty.
2. The light of knowing gives us the power to see intellectual beauty.
3. The Light of God in us gives us the power to see God's Beauty.

Source Material for Book One

These steps are given in BOOK ONE, pages 31–33.
The development continues thus (pages 33 and 34) in three more steps:

1. When the sunlight helps me to see the beautiful things that God has made, I choose them.
2. When my light of knowing gives me the power to see the beauty of my mother's goodness, I love it.
3. When God's Light gives me the power to see His Beauty, I love Him.

In Topic Two the first point that is taught about the effect of grace is that it gives the power to know and love God Himself. The second effect taught is that God loves tenderly a soul in which the Light of Grace is shining.

The third effect is that the presence of grace in a soul makes the one who possesses it a child of God. With this truth established, the parallel truth that God is the Loving Father of everyone who is in the state of grace is also established.

To form an apperceptive basis for teaching that grace is not a right but a gift, ideas of some great gifts given at Creation must be developed in the child's mind.

Beginning with familiar knowledge, the idea that the body is a wonderful gift from God is developed. After that some other wonderful gifts which are not like any part of the body may be taught.

These gifts are the powers of the soul: the power to know and the power to choose. After the powers of the soul are taught, the name "soul" is given. When the topic is finished, the child should know that he is a creature composed of body and soul, which is the first part of the answer to the Catechism question: "What is man?"

The following are the points of application:

1. A Bible verse establishes the fact that God is King of all the earth.
2. All who have the Light of Grace shining in their souls are noble princes and princesses of God's kingdom for they are very dear children of the King of all the earth.
3. A noble prince or princess must love God, his King.
4. One who loves his King will think about Him and pray often during the day.
5. A prince or princess of God's kingdom should be recognized by his actions. He should be brave, kind, and true.
6. God is our Protector and our Shield.
7. A prayer to be brave, kind, and true is given.
8. Bible quotations about children of the Light are introduced.
9. Bible verses are set to Gregorian Chant and melody.

TOPIC THREE: THE ONE WHOSE POWER CAN PROTECT ALL PEOPLE

Topic Three develops the ideas of God's might and power through Old Testament stories, thus leading the child to understand the meaning of the statement, "God is Almighty."

The points of application are

1. A Bible verse from the Canticle of Moses.
2. The development of the first article of the Apostles' Creed: I believe in God, the Father Almighty, the Creator of heaven and earth.
3. The development of the first three petitions of The Lord's Prayer: Hallowed be Thy Name; Thy kingdom come; Thy will be done on earth as it is in heaven.
4. Bible verses appropriate to the lesson set to music.

TOPIC FOUR: THE ONE WHOSE LIGHT CAN SOLVE THE
PROBLEMS OF ALL PEOPLE

In Topic Four the idea that God is All-knowing is developed through a series of stories showing that God knows what everyone is thinking, choosing, saying, and doing. The points of application are

1. The effect upon ourselves of the fact that God sees all things.
2. Practical problems from child life used to bring out points of honor.
3. The development of the last four petitions of The Lord's Prayer: Give us this day our daily bread; and forgive us our trespasses as we forgive those who trespass against us; and lead us not into temptation, but deliver us from evil. Amen.
4. Appropriate Bible verses set to music.

The Catechism statement "God is everywhere" refers to the natural and not to the supernatural presence of God.

The natural presence of God in created things is explained by St. Thomas in the following words:

> He is present in three ways: "By *His power*, by *His presence*, and by *His essence*. By *His power*, because all things are subject to His sovereign command. He is present everywhere, like a king who, while residing in his palace, is by a fiction deemed present in all the parts of his kingdom where he exercises authority. By *His presence*, that is to say, most intimately, because He knows all things and sees all things; and nothing, however hidden it may be, can escape his attention; all things are present to him as objects are said to be in our presence, although they may be situated at a slight distance from our person. Finally by *His essence*, for He is as really and in His very substance present to all created things as a monarch is present in person to the throne on which he is seated."

For any mind untrained in philosophy and particularly for children's minds, it is difficult to distinguish the border line between God's natural presence by His essence and power in all things and pantheistic ideas concerning God's presence in creatures.

So in *The Spiritual Way* series the child is taught that God sees and knows all things. Thus God is everywhere by His presence or by His knowledge. Taught in this way, the child is prepared to receive the knowledge that God is a spirit infinitely perfect; he is ready for the knowledge that God is infinite Intellect and infinite Will. That God is infinite Intellect and infinite Will is taught in *The Spiritual Way*, BOOK THREE, pages 6 and 7.

The natural as well as the supernatural presence of God is discussed in *The Indwelling of the Holy Spirit in the Souls of the Just* by the Reverend Barthelemy Froget, O.P. The natural presence is discussed in Part One of that volume.

Additional projects, tests, and problems for BOOK ONE are given on pages 92, 93, and 100–107.

BOOK TWO

TOPIC FIVE: GOD'S IMAGE AND LIKENESS IN US

The aim of Topic Five is to teach the meaning of the statement: "Man is made to the image and likeness of God." Before teaching it, the teacher should be sure that he knows its meaning as expressed by the Doctors of the Church.

To find the mind of the Church on this point of doctrine, considerable time would have to be spent in research. So for the convenience of teachers, quotations from some of the theologians are given here.

> As man is said to be to the image of God by reason of his intellectual nature, he is the most perfectly like God according to that in which he can best imitate God in his intellectual nature.

Now, the intellectual nature imitates God chiefly in this, that God understands and loves Himself. Wherefore, we see that the image of God is in man in three ways. Firstly, inasmuch as man possesses a natural aptitude for understanding and loving God, which aptitude consists in the very nature of the mind, which is common to all men; secondly, inasmuch as man actually or habitually knows and loves God, though imperfectly, which kind of image is by the conformity of Grace; thirdly, inasmuch as man knows and loves God perfectly, which is from the likeness and conformity of glory. Summa of St. Thomas.

Man is called the image of God, not that he is essentially an image, but that the image of God is impressed on his mind — as a coin is an image of the king, as having the image of the king. Wherefore there is no need to consider the image of God as existing in every part of man. Summa of St. Thomas.

The rational creature is alone capable of beatitude; made to his Creator's image, he was formed for adhering to God, whose image he is. This is the one good of the rational creature, for, as David sings: "My good is to adhere to God." It is not the body but the soul that adheres to God, Who has planted three powers in her, through which she may be the recipient of eternity, the partaker of wisdom, the enjoyer of sweetness. These powers are memory, understanding, and will or love. The man created in these three powers to the image of the Trinity had his memory retentive of God without forgetfulness, his understanding given to know God without error, and his love embracing God without cupidity for other things. And so he was blessed. St. Ælred of Rivaux.

That Blessed and Eternal Trinity, the one God, Father, Son, and Holy Ghost, the Supreme Power, Wisdom, and Benignity, created to His Own image and likeness, a certain trinity in the rational soul, which bears a resemblance to the Supreme Trinity. This resemblance consists in the memory, understanding, and will. God created the soul in this form to abide in Him and partake from Him, that man might be happy. St. Bernard.

The soul is also an image of the Blessed Trinity in virtue of its three powers: memory, understanding, and will. In its memory, it resembles the Father; in its understanding, the Son; and in its will, the Holy

The Spiritual Way: Manual

Ghost. As these three powers are united in one soul, so the three persons of the Blessed Trinity are united in one and the same nature. Notice the words used at the Creation: " Let us make man," thereby indicating the plurality of persons in the Blessed Trinity. It is its likeness to the Blessed Trinity that gives to every single soul its priceless value; it is this which explains the Incarnation.

The body of man is not made in the image of God, for God is a pure spirit, but yet the likeness of God stamps itself in some way on the body, as being the instrument of the soul, both in its upright bearing and in the dominion it asserts over the irrational animals (see Psalm 8 : 5–7). " What is man that thou art mindful of him ? . . . thou hast crowned him with glory and honour : and hast set him over the works of thy hands." REVEREND FRANCIS SPIRAGO in *The Catechism Explained*.

Considerable research in connection with this point of doctrine shows that the majority of theologians give as powers of the soul the memory, the mind, and the will; but St. Thomas gives only the two powers of mind and will. In Topic Five the development is based on the idea of St. Thomas, that the powers of the soul are the mind and the will.

In Topic Two the child was led to realize that he has the power to think and to know and the power to love and to choose. In Topic Five the child's knowledge is advanced by the facts that he thinks and knows with his mind and that he loves and chooses with his will.

Actual experience in using the lessons of Topic Five in experimentation over a period of ten years proved beyond question not only that the child grasps the matter taught but furthermore that it is very satisfying to the child's mind to know just what the powers of his soul are and what he does with them. This has frequently been evidenced when a child who has been taught what he can do with his soul is placed in a position where it is necessary to make a choice. After making the choice, he enjoys the realization that it is his soul that gave him the power to choose.

On page 10 of BOOK TWO (Topic Five) there is a heading "The Turning of the Mind and Will toward God." Under this heading the child is taught the effect of grace upon the mind and the will. The theology back of this is based upon the teachings of St. Augustine and St. Thomas.

St. Thomas says in the Summa:

> Now God moves man's soul by turning it to Himself. . . . Hence for the justification of the ungodly a movement of the mind is required, by which it is turned to God. Now the first turning to God is by faith, according to Hebrews 11 : 6: "He that cometh to God must believe that He is." Hence a movement of faith is required for the justification of the ungodly.
>
> The movement of faith is not perfect unless it is quickened by charity; hence in the justification of the ungodly, a movement of charity is infused together with the movement of faith. Now free will is moved to God by being subject to Him.

A quotation from the *Treatise on Grace* by St. Thomas is this:

> And thus the human understanding has a form, namely, intelligible light, which of itself is sufficient for knowing certain intelligible things, namely, those we can come to know through the senses. Higher intelligible things the human intellect cannot know, unless it be perfected by a stronger light, namely, the light of faith or prophecy, which is called the *light of grace*, inasmuch as it is added to nature.

St. Thomas also says in the Summa:

> In the state of perfect nature man referred the love of himself and of all other things to the love of God as to its end; and thus he loved God more than himself and above all things. But in the state of corrupt nature

man falls short of this in the appetite of his rational will, which unless it is cured by God's grace, follows its private good, on account of the corruption of nature. . . . In the state of corrupted nature man cannot fulfill all the Divine commandments without healing grace.

In this connection, St. Thomas quotes St. Augustine thus:

> Not only do they know by its light what to do, but by its help they do lovingly what they know.

On page 16 of Topic Five the immortality of the soul is taught. In order to make this point of doctrine a real factor in the spiritual life of the children, they are asked to read the lives of certain persons who were willing to endure great suffering of body for the good of their own souls and other souls. The names given are merely suggestive. Teachers may choose others who, because of particular reasons in their parish, school, or locality, might be of greater interest to the children.

On page 19 under the heading "The Soul Should Rule the Body" problems are given which are within the experience of the child. The teacher can formulate any number of similar problems within the group experience of her particular class. For problems of this type help the child to realize his dignity and responsibility as the master of his own actions.

TOPIC SIX: WHY GOD MADE US TO HIS IMAGE AND LIKENESS

The aim of Topic Six is to teach the statement of the Catechism: "God made me to know Him, to love Him, and to serve Him in this world."

As this Catechism statement expresses the purpose of our

creation, it is well worth while to take the time to develop each of these points carefully and thoroughly so that the child will really know what is expected of him. St. Ignatius, a great master of the spiritual life, makes this a fundamental subject of serious meditation for all who wish to advance spiritually.

If the purpose of our creation is well taught, the child should leave the study of Topic Six with a foundation laid for the development of a solid spiritual life. Many difficult moral problems might disappear if the child knew very early in life the fundamental point of doctrine that God is actually dwelling within souls in the state of grace. So this doctrine is taught as a point of application in Topic Six, on page 40. The child knows that at Baptism the Light of Grace came into his soul. And he should be taught that his first concern should be so to live that he will remain in the state of grace and thus keep God living within his soul.

Another point of application in Topic Six is that we must believe in God, hope in Him, and love Him with all our heart. In teaching this statement, we use Acts of Faith, Hope, Love, and Contrition. The Acts are given on pages 44–47.

Pope Clement XI's Acts are used because it has been found, after testing the experience of many adults, that the Acts which they habitually say are always short and simple. It has also been found after considerable testing that many who have not been taught short acts omit the Acts of Faith, Hope, and Love entirely.

TOPIC SEVEN: THE KINGDOM OF NOBLEST PRINCES AND PRINCESSES

In Topic Seven the title " The Kingdom of Noblest Princes and Princesses " is used instead of the usual heading " Heaven," because this title is a challenge. The familiar word " heaven " would not arouse the children's interest, as they are likely to feel that there is nothing new to learn about it.

Heaven

In Topic Seven the idea of heaven is presented to the child as a gift instead of as a reward. The children know that grace is the most precious gift they have received from God, and that as long as the Light of Grace is shining in their souls they belong in heaven with God. The logical conclusion from teaching grace as a gift is to teach heaven as a gift.

The following are the essential points brought out in the presentation of heaven.

1. Perfect union with God forever is secured.

This is expressed by the sentence, " God will take you to Himself forever," on page 54.

The Catechism of the Council of Trent expresses this idea in these words:

> The only means, then, of arriving at a knowledge of the Divine Essence is that God unites Himself in some sort to us, and after an incomprehensible manner elevates our minds to a higher degree of perfection, and thus renders us capable of contemplating the beauty of His nature. This the light of His glory will accomplish.

2. Union with God requires absolute purity.

This is expressed by the sentence beginning on page 53,

Source Material for Book Two   41

"When your soul leaves the body, if God's image and likeness in your soul are as clear and perfect as God wants them to be, He will take you to Himself forever."

3. Union with God in heaven gives everlasting happiness.

This is expressed by the sentence on page 54, "When Our Heavenly Father takes you to Himself, you will be happy forever."

4. Union with God means the absence of everything opposed to happiness.

This is expressed on page 54 by the sentence, "You will never have any more sickness, or sufferings, or death."

5. The term "heaven" is given on page 54 after the preceding four points have been taught, and with it the idea that in heaven everyone will be forever in an atmosphere of love, first through God's Love, and then through that of all the saints. Also on page 54 heaven is taught as the greatest of all God's priceless gifts to us, because it gives us God Himself forever.

6. What St. Paul says about heaven (1 Corinthians 2:9) is presented.

7. Finally it is taught on page 55 that the chief reason why God made us is that we may be happy with Him in heaven. This is the completion of the Catechism statement taught in Topic Six, "God made us to know, to love, and to serve Him in this world, and to be happy with Him forever in heaven."

Hell

Heaven is the end for which we were created and hell is the missing of that end. So the textbook presents the end as the main topic and then the failure to reach that end.

The following are the essential points brought out in the presentation of the idea of hell beginning on page 57.
 1. People who refuse to know, to love, and to serve God are unwise.
 2. Even here on earth grace can be lost.
 3. The effects of the loss of grace on the mind and will during life are
    a. The mind is darkened, so that it does not see God's Beauty.
    b. The will is turned away from God.
 These effects are taught by St. Thomas in the Summa:

> By mortal sin, the mind through acting against charity is altogether turned away from God; whereas by venial sin man's affections are clogged so that they are slow in tending towards God.
> Consequently both kinds of sin are taken away by penance because by both of them man's will is disordered through turning inordinately to a created good. For just as mortal sin cannot be forgiven so long as the will is attached to sin, so neither can venial sin, because while the cause remains, the effect remains.

 4. The condition of the mind and will after death if the Light of Grace is not shining in the soul is
    a. The mind must remain forever darkened.
    b. The will must remain forever turned away from God.
 5. The loss of hope is taught on page 58.
 6. The term "hell" is introduced.
 7. The companionship with the devils is noted on page 58.
 8. The everlasting suffering of hell is taught.
 9. The fire of hell is discussed.
 10. The story of Lazarus and Dives is given.

Source Material for Book Two

Purgatory

There is a difference of opinion among theologians as to the nature of that purification which the souls undergo in purgatory. From what are they purified? From the guilt of sin, or simply from imperfections? If from imperfections, in what sense do they become perfect? In that they are intrinsically improved; or is it merely that they have bettered their condition before God?

Bellarmine goes so far as to maintain that the *culpa* or guilt of venial sin is remitted in purgatory. . . . He says that the true opinion is St. Thomas's, that the guilt of venial sin, *culpas veniales*, is remitted in purgatory by an act of love and patient endurance.

Suarez, on the other hand, does not seem to admit that purgatory betters the soul in any other sense than enabling it to discharge the debt of punishment due to sin. . . .

On the whole, there does not appear anything contrary to sound theology in the idea of such an intrinsic improvement taking place in the soul in purgatory as is implied in the gradual getting rid of passive bad habits and earthly tastes. From the Appendix of a translation of ST. CATHERINE OF GENOA'S *Treatise on Purgatory.*

Whosoever comes into God's presence must be perfectly pure, for in the strictest sense His " eyes are too pure to behold evil " (Habacuc 1 : 13). For unrepented venial faults, for the payment of temporal punishment due to sin at the time of death, the Church has always taught the doctrine of purgatory. EDWARD J. HANNA, S.T.D. in the article on " Purgatory " in *The Catholic Encyclopedia.*

But still I see that the Being of God is so pure (far more than one can imagine), that should a soul see in itself even the least note of imperfection, it would rather cast itself into a thousand hells than go with that spot into the presence of the Divine Majesty. Therefore, seeing purgatory ordained to take away such blemishes, it plunges therein, and deems it a great mercy that it can thus remove them.

Gold which has been purified to a certain point ceases to suffer any diminution from the action of fire, however great it may be; for the fire does not destroy gold, but only the dross that it may chance to have.

In like manner the Divine fire acts on souls: God holds them in the furnace until every defect has been burned away, and He has brought them, each in his own degree, to a certain standard of perfection. ST. CATHERINE OF GENOA in *The Treatise on Purgatory.*

In this Topic the discussion of purgatory is begun. In Topic Nine, " Untrue Princes and Princesses " (page 115 of BOOK TWO), the discussion is continued; and in Topic Seventeen, " The Font of Mercy " (page 115 of BOOK FOUR), the discussion of purgatory is completed.

Heaven is the end for which we were created and hell is the missing of that end; if the end is not fully attained at death, purgatory is the means of attaining it.

The following are the essential points brought out in the presentation of purgatory, beginning on page 61.

1. Because of the absolute purity of God, nothing that is defiled can enter heaven.

2. If the soul is not as pure as God wants it to be, it cannot be in heaven immediately after death.

3. The soul must wait and suffer until it is pure enough to be with God.

4. The constant longing of the soul to be in heaven with God is its greatest suffering.

5. The term " purgatory " and its meaning are given on page 62.

The doctrine of the Communion of Saints, Guardian Angels, the Commandments of the New Law, and the first five Commandments of the Old Law are taught as applications of this Topic.

There are several questions on the first five Commandments given in the Baltimore Catechism No. 2 which are not developed in *The Spiritual Way.* There are also a number of Topics developed in *The Spiritual Way* which are not given in the Catechism.

Question 323, concerning heretics and infidels, has been omitted. A careful development of this question, which seems too complex for this period, would be necessary to give the child the right Christian attitude toward those who are not members of the Catholic Church.

Questions 327-329 treat of presumption and despair. For spiritual growth, the virtue of confidence should be developed. But it is difficult for a child to grasp the difference between confidence and presumption. In *The Spiritual Way* this point is taught by suggestion rather than in a formal way. For throughout several Topics, especially Topics One and Ten, an attitude of humility and reverence is established. Where humility and reverence exist, presumption cannot.

The meaning of the sin of despair would be difficult for a little child to grasp; but if the teacher considers it advisable to teach this point, the story of Judas would form a good apperceptive basis.

One of the best ways of checking the child's understanding of the Commandments is by means of tests and problems. A test and a problem are given here as suggestions to the teacher, who can formulate many others based on the Commandments.

A Test: Honoring Images and Relics

Copy Groups I and II in your Project Book.

Read the first statement in Group I. Then find the statement in Group II which explains it. Put the number of the explanation in the parenthesis before the statement in Group I. Do the same with the other statements and explanations.

The Spiritual Way: Manual

Group I: Statements

( ) It was the feast of the patron saint of the Church. The congregation came to honor a relic of the saint. They did not break the first Commandment.

( ) Jennie said her prayers before an altar in her room, on which was a crucifix and a statue of the Blessed Virgin. She knew that the crucifix and the statue could not help her in any other way than by reminding her of Jesus and His Blessed Mother.

( ) There is a crucifix on every altar.

Group II: Explanations

1. The first Commandment does not forbid the use of images to remind us of Jesus, His Blessed Mother, and the saints.

2. The crucifix and the cross remind us of the cruel death of Jesus.

3. The first Commandment does not forbid us to honor authentic relics of Our Lord or of His saints.

The correct answers are

Group I		Group II
1	is explained by	3
2	is explained by	1
3	is explained by	2

In the Catechism the subject of oaths and vows is presented in connection with the study of the second Commandment. No detailed development of oaths is necessary for small children, but some practical problems like the following could be given.

John's father saw an accident. He was ordered to appear in court and tell about the accident. He took an oath to tell the truth about what he saw. What Commandment says that it is lawful to take an oath when it is ordered by lawful authority?

If the children are older and have some knowledge of civics and civil courts, this subject may be more fully developed.

It seems unwise to develop the subject of vows with young children. The Catechism statement is probably all that can be wisely given.

TOPIC EIGHT: THE FAILURE OF THE FIRST NOBLE PRINCE AND PRINCESS

The subject of Topic Eight is original sin. A series of lessons on original sin is not generally attractive to child or adult and requires a carefully prepared presentation to arouse and sustain interest.

Instead of "Original Sin," the title of this Topic is "The Failure of the First Noble Prince and Princess." This correlates with the preceding title and is designed to arouse the child's curiosity.

The basic or underlying idea of original sin in its first cause is disobedience to God and disregard for His law. So the apperceptive basis used for this Topic is the consequences of disregarding natural laws. The child, knowing that suffering follows the breaking of natural laws, is given a mental urge to find out what kind of suffering followed when God's law was broken for the first time. The child must, of course, be told the story of the disobedience of Adam as the head of the human race. In order to establish an interesting background for this lesson, the story is first given in the form of an allegory, and to give added interest a puzzle element is introduced.

The stern fact is brought home to the child that the head of the human race broke God's law, thus committing sin; and the sufferings which followed the breaking of this law are told. He sees that the gifts which Adam no longer had could not become the inheritance of the race. It is then quite clear why the Light of Grace is not shining in the soul of each child born into this world. This is not a new idea to the children, for most of them know from observation or experience that if the father of a family loses money or property he cannot leave this to be inherited by his family.

The doctrine of original sin is presented first as a loss of grace. After that, the child will have a background for the interpretation of original sin as inherited sin.

As an application of Topic Seven, the first five Commandments of the Old Law were taught. The sixth Commandment is taught as an application of Topic Eight.

The sixth Commandment was given by God, just as the other Commandments were. Therefore, we have the same obligation to teach this Commandment as the others.

Because of the present social conditions and their effect on the mental attitude and moral life of present-day society, our Catholic Christian Doctrine teachers cannot afford to be negative in their attitude toward the vital moral and spiritual questions involved in the sixth Commandment. This teaching is being handled on a natural and scientific basis by many teachers of subjects other than Christian Doctrine. But children need more than scientific knowledge to help them to lead a pure life. So the child should have the matter presented from a supernatural point of view.

For the knowledge that " the temple of God is holy, which you are " will lay a foundation of reverence for God's temple and of holy fear of any thought, word, or action which would offend the Master dwelling within the temple.

Sometimes in working with groups of children it may be discovered that wrong physical habits have been formed through ignorance while the child was very young. Then it is necessary that his mind be informed concerning its duty as the guardian of God's sacred temple, and he should know that both his mind and his will must be strengthened by grace in order to overcome such physical tendencies.

The sixth Commandment is "Thou shalt not commit adultery." So in order to teach this Commandment, it is first necessary to teach the meaning of the term "adultery." There is grave danger that if this Commandment is not taught fully, the child will not know what is a sin and what is not a sin.

In order to teach the meaning of adultery, it has seemed necessary to distinguish between the married state and the virgin state. This distinction is carefully presented in Topic Eight.

The child must also understand that according to the teaching of the Church the sixth Commandment may be broken by other sins than adultery. This is explained under the heading "The Master of the Temple" on page 97 after the child has been taught the meaning of purity and holiness, which is presented on page 94.

It is our duty to lead the child to understand that if he keeps his mind and will turned toward God, he will know where there is danger of lessening or losing the purity and holiness of his soul, and he will be able to decide the best thing to do to avoid or overcome the danger. This is presented on pages 98–102.

It will be noted that during the entire presentation of the sixth Commandment the mind of the child is kept constantly turned toward God and His Presence. The result of this teaching will be a realization of the Presence of God, in the light of which the child will be able to solve his moral problems correctly.

Topic Nine: Untrue Princes and Princesses

As heaven, our true destiny, is presented under the heading " A Kingdom of Noblest Princes and Princesses," it is in keeping with this setting to present mortal and venial sin under the heading " Untrue Princes and Princesses."

In Topic Six the children memorized Acts of Faith, Hope, Love, and Contrition. They also learned that it is necessary, in order to attain the end for which we were created, that we believe in God, hope in Him, and love Him. At the beginning of Topic Nine attention is called to the Catechism statement that in order to save our souls we must worship God by Faith, Hope, and Love.

In this Topic it is shown how unhappiness may result from the way we use our wills to choose.

The first man used his will to choose to disobey God and thus to commit sin. Very great unhappiness followed this choice.

We can choose to disobey God. Great unhappiness will follow such a choice.

In *The Spiritual Way* the results of Adam's choosing and the results of our choosing are presented.

The Results of Adam's Choosing to Disobey God

After Adam chose to disobey God:
    (a) The Light of Grace was not then shining in his soul.
    (b) He did not then belong in Our Heavenly Father's kingdom.

Source Material for Book Two

(c) He lost his gift of clear knowledge; his mind was darkened.
(d) His will was weakened and turned away from God.
(e) It was not easy for his mind and his will to rule his body.

It is generally supposed that because of Adam's deep contrition and great suffering during hundreds of years God let him again share in the Light of Grace. If God had not let him share in the Light of Grace once more, Adam would have had to suffer in hell forever.

The Effect of Adam's Choice upon the Human Race

Because Adam, the head of the human race, chose to refuse the great gift of sharing in Divine Life:

(a) The Light of Grace is not shining in our souls when we are born.
(b) We are not children of God's heavenly kingdom when we are born.
(c) Our minds are darkened so that we never see things as clearly as Adam saw them before his sin.
(d) Our wills are weakened and always inclined to turn away from God.
(e) It is not easy for our minds and our wills to rule our bodies.
(f) If God does not give us the Light of Grace before we die, we cannot be united with Him in heaven.

The Results of Our Choosing to Commit a Mortal Sin

After Baptism, if anyone chooses to commit a mortal sin:

(a) The Light of Grace will not then be shining in his soul.
(b) He does not then belong in heaven with God.
(c) His mind becomes still more darkened as to the things of God.
(d) His will is turned away from God.
(e) It is more difficult for his mind and will to rule his body.
(f) If he dies in the state of mortal sin, he must suffer in hell forever.

The Results of Our Choosing to Commit Venial Sins

When anyone in the state of grace chooses to commit venial sins:

(a) His will becomes weaker.
(b) He is more likely to commit a mortal sin.

(c) He does not love God as perfectly as he is capable of loving Him.
(d) He is likely to forfeit blessings which he would otherwise receive.
(e) He brings suffering upon himself, for suffering follows every sin.
(f) He may have to suffer after death in purgatory.

The seventh, eighth, ninth, and tenth Commandments are taught as applications of this Topic. It will be noted that in *The Spiritual Way* the Commandments are not presented as a topic by themselves but as applications of points of doctrine.

As in Topic Seven, problems are given as one of the best ways of testing the child's understanding of the Commandments. The teacher may formulate additional problems.

Additional projects, tests, and problems for BOOK TWO are given on pages 93–96 and 107–113.

BOOK THREE

TOPIC TEN: THE BLESSED TRINITY

As a preparation for teaching the Blessed Trinity, a good foundation of humility must be laid by helping the child to realize that all created minds are limited in power.

To prepare the child's mind for the acceptance of supernatural mysteries, his attention is called to familiar natural mysteries. Then he is taught that without faith it is impossible to please God.

In previous lessons the child learned that the mind and the will are powers of the soul, but he has not yet been taught that the soul is a spirit. In Topic Ten he learns that the soul is a spirit, angels are spirits, and God is a spirit. And the word " spirit " is not given as a mere term; its meaning is carefully developed.

Source Material for Book Three

It will be noted that great care has been taken in the use of the terms *mind* and *will*. When these terms are used with reference to the human soul, they are spoken of as powers of the soul. But when they are used with reference to God, we do not speak of them as powers, for, to quote directly from St. Thomas, " The Essence of God is His Intellect and Will." The exact phraseology of St. Thomas is used in *The Spiritual Way:* " In God there exists Intellect and Will " and "God acts by His Intellect and Will."

With the mind of the child thus carefully prepared, the great mystery of the Blessed Trinity is presented. In teaching the idea of the Trinity, we may use various devices. In Topic Ten the shamrock has been chosen as being the most familiar and therefore the most easily grasped by the child mind.

A lesson on the Blessed Trinity would be incomplete without the Athanasian Creed. Some lines of this Creed are given on page 13 of BOOK THREE, but a teacher may wish to use more of this " greatest hymn of praise." Cardinal Newman, recognizing the value of the Athanasian Creed and the beauty of the way in which it expresses the doctrines of faith, enthusiastically calls it the "greatest war song of faith."

Time could not be better spent than in memorizing some lines from the Athanasian Creed, for they will give the child definite truth in a very pleasing way.

As an application of the lesson on the Holy Trinity, the Sign of the Cross is taught as an Act of Faith when said thoughtfully and with reverence. The Catechism statements concerning prayer are developed by means of the dialogue on page 16. This seems a living way of bringing home to the child a rather difficult point.

The special work attributed to each Person of the Blessed Trinity is stated, but in a book for young children it seemed best to omit the processions.

In Topic Six, on page 49 of BOOK TWO, the children learned that most important and fundamental truth of Catholic faith, the indwelling of the Holy Ghost in souls in the state of grace. This doctrine is enlarged upon in Topic Ten.

Problems and projects are used in the text to bring home to the child the reality of the indwelling and its effect upon his everyday life.

The headings in connection with this development are

> The Great Lover of Our Souls
> The God-Bearer
> Elizabeth of the Trinity
> Making a Retreat

TOPIC ELEVEN: JESUS, GOD AND MAN

The aim of this Topic is to teach the child how it came about that, although we were born in the state of original sin, God lets us share in the Light of His Grace by means of Baptism.

The child is led to see that after the first mortal sin our first parents were in the power of the devil, and they knew that they could not free themselves from the devil's power. But God's great promise of a Redeemer gave them hope in the midst of their unhappy condition.

The coming of the Redeemer is then presented, and the main points in His life are given.

After the discussion of the General Judgment on page 42, the following Bible verses might be taught.

Source Material for Book Three

What doth it profit a man, if he gain the whole world, and suffer the loss of his own soul? Or what exchange shall a man give for his soul? For the Son of man shall come in the glory of His Father with His angels: and then will he render to every man according to his works. (St. Matthew 16: 26, 27.)

As an application of the Topic "Jesus, God and Man," the second part of the Apostles' Creed is presented. The child should be asked to find in the Catechism the explanation of the article of the Apostles' Creed which says, "sitteth at the right hand of God, the Father Almighty."

The child is taught explicitly and carefully how to use the New Testament and is directed to look up many references concerning the life of Jesus. The difference between the New Testament and other books which tell about the life of Jesus is also taught.

At this period of the child's instruction he should be given the opportunity to become acquainted with *The Following of Christ*, also called *The Imitation of Christ*. He should understand the place that this book holds among spiritual books and should also be shown the value of its frequent and intelligent use as an impetus to his spiritual life. The practical use of *The Imitation* with many children has proved that it is within the comprehension of childhood.

In Topic Eleven the child is given a knowledge of the meaning of the feasts of the Church in honor of Jesus, God and Man. The spiritual purpose of the parish societies should also be taught here. Two feasts and two societies are introduced as types in Topic Eleven. The feasts are the Feast of the Sacred Heart of Jesus and the Feast of the Kingship of Our Lord Jesus Christ. The societies are the Holy Name Society and the League of the Sacred Heart.

The meaning of the three terms, " the Image of the Father," " the Word," and " the Light of the World," are explained to the child.

TOPIC TWELVE: MARY, MOTHER OF JESUS

The heading of Topic Twelve is " Mary, Mother of Jesus." The familiar term " the Blessed Virgin Mary " is explained at the beginning of this Topic.

The dogma of the Immaculate Conception is carefully and clearly presented to the child.

When children are allowed merely to memorize the definition of the Immaculate Conception, they are likely to go through life with a misunderstanding of this important dogma and also to explain this doctrine incorrectly, thus leaving an entirely false impression.

In the teaching of this lesson, the Conception of the Mother of Christ celebrated on the Feast of the Immaculate Conception should not be confused with the birth of Christ celebrated on the Feast of the Nativity.

As a point of interest closely associated with this Topic, teachers in the United States of America should tell the children that the Feast of the Immaculate Conception is the patronal feast of the United States. The children should be taught also about the National Shrine at Washington, D. C., in honor of the Immaculate Conception. Pictures of Our Lady of Washington and well-known pictures of the Immaculate Conception should be shown.

The life of the Blessed Virgin Mary is taught in the textbook in the form of story puzzles. These story puzzles will be interesting to the child and will help to give an attractive setting.

Source Material for Book Three

As an application of this Topic, the Hail Mary, the Rosary, the Memorare, and Hail, Holy Queen are developed.

The principal feast days of the Blessed Virgin are taught.

On page 85 of this Topic theological reasons for honoring the Blessed Virgin Mary are given. On page 93 some poetic ways of honoring the Blessed Virgin based upon the color blue are suggested because the form used here has been found to make a strong appeal to the child.

TOPIC THIRTEEN: THE SACRIFICES OF THE OLD LAW

The Sacrifices of the Old Law and why they were acceptable to God are an apperceptive basis for the study of the Holy Sacrifice of the Mass. The Feast of the Passover is taught as basic to the understanding of the history of the first Mass. The idea that the blood of a lamb sprinkled on the doorposts saved the lives of the chosen people is brought before the child to prepare his mind to receive the great truth that God planned to save the world through the Blood of Jesus, the true Lamb.

In this Topic the fact that the New Law is the completion and fulfillment of the Old Law is clearly presented to the child. He is also made to understand that the efficacy of the sacrifices of the Old Law lay in the fact that they were ordered by God and carried out exactly as He prescribed.

Texts from the Old Testament are used freely to bring out these points. The story of Abraham's offering his only son Isaac in sacrifice prepares the mind to receive the great truth that the Father sent His only begotten Son to be offered in Sacrifice for the salvation of the world. The child is led to see that great things depended upon Abraham's obedience to God and also that great things may depend upon the child's obedience to Him.

The test on pages 112 and 113 of BOOK THREE is used to show that the great men of the Old Law obeyed God's commands and offered sacrifice.

Father Keith's Famous Mass Pictures

These pictures, consisting of one hundred lantern slides and stereographs prepared by the Reverend George A. Keith, S.J., show in a true and perfect way the development and the construction of the Holy Sacrifice of the Mass. These pictures evidence years of research in developing to the highest degree every detail from the artistic, historical, and theological standpoints. They can be secured from The Keystone View Company, Meadville, Pennsylvania.

Father Keith will give personal attention to anyone who desires further information about these slides or the lectures which he gives on the Holy Sacrifice of the Mass, using the slides. His national headquarters are Loyola University, Chicago, Illinois.

TOPIC FOURTEEN: THE HOLY SACRIFICE OF THE MASS

The foundation for this Topic has been carefully laid in the preceding Topic on the sacrifices of the Old Law. Topic Fourteen begins with the presentation of the last Passover celebrated by Jesus. Again the truth is brought before the child's mind that God is the Author of the Old Law as well as the New, and that the New Law is the fulfillment of the Old.

The story of the preparation for the Passover celebration by Jesus and the Apostles is given to the children in the form of a test, with the idea of impressing the details more forcibly upon their minds. The heading "The Sacrificial Lamb of the New Law," on page 118, immediately forms the link between the sacrificial lambs of the Old Law and the Sacrificial Lamb of the New Law.

Prophecies from Isaias, concerning the lamb-like qualities of Jesus, the true Lamb, are presented to the child for consideration.

A test given on pages 120 and 121 shows that the characteristics of the lamb foretold by Isaias are fulfilled in the life of Jesus, as written in the New Testament.

Under the heading "The Unbloody Sacrifice of the New Law," it is impressed upon the child that it was God Himself Who made known that sacrifice is the form of worship most acceptable to Him in both the Old Law and the New Law. Under this heading the story of the Last Supper and the doctrine of transubstantiation are presented. The term "transubstantiation" is omitted, but with many classes it would be most desirable for the teacher to use this term.

Under the heading "Do This for a Commemoration of Me" (page 124), the power of consecration given to the priesthood is taught. This text is explained in the following quotation:

> In the following words: "Do this for a commemoration of me," the Lord commandeth His Apostles and their successors in the priestly dignity to do the same as He had done, until His return at the end of time, that is, continually to offer the Eucharistic Sacrifice which He had just offered in their presence. By this command, as a natural consequence, He also imparted to them the power of consecration, or of offering sacri-

fice, that is, He made them priests of the New Law. Thus our Lord instituted the Eucharistic Sacrifice, and willed to transmit the power to offer it to priests only, to whom it appertains to partake of it and to distribute it to the rest. The REVEREND NICHOLAS GIHR in *The Holy Sacrifice of the Mass.*

The treatise by Dr. Gihr on the Holy Sacrifice of the Mass is very complete. Any teacher who wishes to give the children an understanding of the value of the Mass and an appreciation for it will find the book a very valuable and helpful aid.

Under the next heading the child is taught that official sacrifice, in either the Old or the New Law, must be offered by a priest. On the Cross, Jesus was our great High Priest and here He offered the only bloody Sacrifice of the New Law. From that time on Jesus' priests have represented Him in offering the unbloody Sacrifice of the New Law.

As the Eternal High Priest according to the order of Melchisedech, Christ does not and will not cease until the consummation of time to offer Himself in the Mass to His Heavenly Father; but now He no longer does so alone in a personal, visible manner, as He did at the Last Supper and upon the Cross, but invisibly and with the assistance of a human representative. Christ is indeed the principal celebrant at the altar, for He has the primary and chief part in the celebration of the Eucharistic Sacrifice; still He does not perform this action alone and without assistance, but employs for it specially authorized servants and instruments, namely, validly ordained priests. The REVEREND NICHOLAS GIHR in *The Holy Sacrifice of the Mass.*

Under the next heading appear the names, "the Holy Sacrifice of the Mass," "the Sacrifice of the Holy Eucharist," and "the Eucharistic Sacrifice." The meaning of the word "Eucharist" and the appropriateness of its use here are carefully explained.

Source Material for Book Three 61

Under the heading "The Continuous Offering of Sacrifice," the prophecy of Malachias (Malachias 1:11) is given.

There are many possible ways of presenting the structure of the Mass and many possible divisions. In Topic Fourteen the Consecration is presented first because it is the central and essential part of the Mass. Then the prayers preceding the Consecration are taught as preparing for this essential part, and the prayers after the Consecration as a thanksgiving for the great Sacrifice which has just taken place.

After the lesson has been completed and while lantern slides of the Mass are being shown, the children should be asked to notice how all the prayers and the movements and gestures of the priest and servers before the Consecration express sentiments of humility, contrition, and self-oblation. They should also be told to notice that during the Consecration the entire atmosphere is one of solemnity and that every exterior movement of priest and people expresses deep reverence, adoration, and love.

The Consecration is followed by prayers of thanksgiving. The slides show that the Sacrifice is ended and that the people are ready to return to their homes with God's blessing upon them.

Since inexpensive editions of Missals are prepared for children, every child should be encouraged to use the Missal intelligently. On page 139 a Missal Hunt is given as a means of making the child familiar with the Missal. It also helps him to appreciate the relative values of the different parts of the Mass and the appropriateness of the prayers, which are filled with the proper sentiments for each part of the Mass.

No lesson on the Mass would be complete without a study of the altar, the altar stone, sacred vessels, linens, and in fact almost everything that is essential to the offering of the Holy Sacrifice of the Mass. This discussion is given on pages 140-144 of BOOK THREE.

BOOK FOUR

TOPIC FIFTEEN: JESUS' CHURCH

To give any true conception of the Church, the guide and teacher established by Christ, it must be presented to the child in its proper historical setting.

It is important for the teacher to understand that, in order to present Topic Fifteen in its true historical and theological setting, he should be familiar with the preceding fourteen topics of *The Spiritual Way* as an apperceptive basis. For to try to teach this Topic on the Church without first establishing the background explaining the reason for its existence as teacher and channel of grace is like building a house without a foundation.

The Church is the true guide and teacher and also the channel through which grace comes to the human race. But how can this twofold office of the Church be adequately taught unless the child has some understanding of what the possession of grace meant to our first parents and what the loss of this priceless gift meant to them and to the whole human race?

A question may arise in the teacher's mind as to why the title "Jesus' Church" is used continually. This is done for two reasons. First, in the pedagogical development the term "the Holy Catholic Church" should come toward the end of the Topic; second, after the Divinity of Christ is established, the term "Jesus' Church" always connotes that the Church is Divine in its origin.

In Topic Fifteen the child's mind is directed at once to Adam's sin and the promise of a Redeemer given in the Garden of Eden.

Then the purpose of the active life of Jesus is briefly reviewed, and the fact is suggested that Jesus had made a plan to carry on His work when He would no longer be on earth. The history of the call of the Apostles, their mission, and the powers given to them, as told in the New Testament, are presented to the children.

Then the further plan for carrying on Jesus' work throughout the ages is presented with closely related Bible texts. Bible texts which show the preëminence of Peter among the Apostles are quoted and developed. There are also beautiful illustrations of the texts. The marks of the Church are given and their meaning is brought home to the child through challenging questions.

As an application of this Topic, the Commandments of the Church are taught through the medium of problems. But the problems in the textbook are merely suggestive. Every teacher should formulate other problems appropriate to the age of the child and the locality in which he teaches.

The doctrine that the Church is the Mystical Body of Christ is developed under the three headings: "The Vine," "The Mystical Body," and "The Corner-Stone."

The Birthday of the Church, its holiness, and its power to sanctify are discussed on pages 31 and 32 of BOOK FOUR under the heading "Jesus Sends the Paraclete." Finally, the doctrine that the Church is "The Infallible Teacher in Faith and Morals" is taught.

Throughout this Topic, Bible texts are given in profusion to show the Biblical origin of the material taught in the lesson.

TOPIC SIXTEEN: THE COMING OF THE LIGHT OF GRACE

The Sacrament of Baptism is discussed in Topic Sixteen under the heading "The Coming of the Light of Grace." This title serves a twofold purpose. First, it links Baptism with the first reception of grace. Second, it challenges the interest of the child, who may think he knows all about Baptism.

The beginning of the lesson brings before the child's mind the connection between the gift of grace and the passion and death of Christ.

To help establish the truth that grace is necessary to the spiritual life and to show the ways in which it reaches the individual soul, grace is compared to water, which is necessary to natural life. A further comparison is then made to the ways in which water reaches the individual in the home. This comparison was chosen because, as is shown on page 46, Jesus Himself compares grace to water.

Then grace, the water of life, is spoken of as coming from a fountain, again using the Biblical comparison. Next the child is led to see that the Church is the Fountain through which grace is distributed and that Jesus is the hidden Source from which the water of life flows.

After a brief general discussion of the Sacraments, the Sacrament of Baptism is presented. Baptism of water, Baptism of desire, and Baptism of blood are discussed.

Other essential subjects which are carefully presented are the attitude of the Church on private Baptism and the duties of godfather and godmother.

The bringing of the Light of Grace to other souls through missionary work, under any of its forms, is one of the strongest applications for the lesson on Baptism. Two international associations are mentioned on page 62, but the teacher may take this opportunity to direct the child's attention to local organizations and to stress the opportunity of the individual in helping to bring Baptism to other souls.

In order that the attention of the child may be directed to the beauty of the ceremonies of Baptism, a portion of this ceremony has been outlined under three headings:

1. What the priest does
2. What the priest says
3. What the one to be baptized or his sponsor says or does

The child is asked to complete the ceremony from a *Manual of Prayers* or other book.

Finally as an application, the last articles of the Apostles' Creed are explained.

TOPIC SEVENTEEN: THE FONT OF MERCY

"The Font of Mercy" is the heading under which the Sacrament of Penance is taught. This heading is used because mercy is the attribute of God which is especially shown in the forgiveness of sin. At the beginning of the Topic two stories showing the mercy of Jesus, God and Man, are told. This places the child in a proper mental attitude for the right understanding of this Sacrament.

Under the heading "The Keys of the Kingdom of Heaven," the symbolism of the key and the meaning of bind and loose are explained. There is also an explanation of the power given to the Apostles and their successors, the priests, on the first Easter Sunday in the Cenacle, when the Sacrament of Penance was established.

Although the child may know the words of the Confiteor and the Act of Contrition, both of these prayers are taught in this Topic to insure greater certainty that he grasps the meaning and is not using mere words.

In all probability the child has been going to Confession for some years, but it seems advisable in studying the Sacrament of Penance to review the manner of going to Confession. This will serve to remove any incorrect ideas that he may have formed and to clarify his ideas so that he knows what to do himself and can tell someone else.

The examination of conscience which was given to the child at the time of receiving First Communion should be replaced here by one more extensive and in keeping with his age. The teacher will notice that, although the Commandments of the Old Law are included in the questions of the examination of conscience, the arrangement and division are based upon the Commandments of the New Law.

In connection with the section "Alone with God" on page 87, when the child is given instructions as to how to examine his conscience, it would be appropriate to explain the subject of *actual grace*. For the child is then being instructed to ask God to enlighten his mind and to move his will so that he will know his sins and be sorry for them. This is an illustration of a petition for a particular actual grace.

It seems appropriate to teach thoroughly the subject of indulgences in connection with the Sacrament of Penance. Our knowledge of history makes it quite clear that the sub-

Source Material for Book Four 67

ject of indulgences is one which must be carefully explained so that the correct Catholic doctrine of indulgences will be thoroughly understood by the Catholic child.

The doctrine of the Communion of Saints is carefully explained in BOOK TWO and these two doctrines are closely interrelated. For this reason, the heading given for the entire discussion of indulgences is " Bearing One Another's Burdens." At the beginning of the discussion, the idea of bearing one another's burdens in ways which the child already knows is reviewed.

The child then reads the statement, " Before learning the third way of bearing one another's burdens, you must know about the order of justice." This is explained by a story which brings out the idea of justice and also the idea that satisfaction must be made for any act of injustice. The fact is taught that all sin causes disorder because it is in opposition to the law of justice established by God. And St. Thomas is quoted to teach the child that the disorder caused by sin must be brought back to order, either in this world or in the next, and that the restoring of the order of justice always causes suffering.

The meaning of temporal punishment, its relation to suffering and also to the penance given by the priest in Confession, is next presented.

The meaning of indulgences could not be taught without explaining quite thoroughly what is meant by the spiritual treasury of the Church. This explanation is given on pages 108 and 109. Under the heading "The Power to Bind and Loose" on page 111, after careful preparation, the meaning of the canonical penances and also the meaning of indulgences is taught.

The power to bind and loose was explained on pages 79 and 80. Now partial and plenary indulgences are explained and also their value in helping to pay the debt of temporal punishment caused by our sins and the sins of others. Finally the value of accepting sufferings as a means of helping to bear the burden of punishment for others, whether living or dead, is explained.

TOPIC EIGHTEEN: THE LIVING BREAD

In Topic Fourteen the Holy Eucharist was taught as a Sacrifice, and Jesus as the Eucharistic Lamb. Now in Topic Eighteen, under the heading "The Living Bread," the Holy Eucharist is taught as a Sacrament, another stream of grace coming to us through the Church, the Fountain of Grace.

St. Thomas says in the Summa: "This Sacrament is both a Sacrifice and a Sacrament; it has the nature of a Sacrifice inasmuch as it is offered up; and it has the nature of a Sacrament inasmuch as it is received."

The child learned, in BOOK ONE, about sanctifying grace as the gift through which we share in God's Light and Beauty, because this means much more to a young child than the more advanced phraseology — "sharing in the Divine Life of God." Either approach to teaching about sanctifying grace conveys the idea that through grace we share in something of God Himself. The idea of grace given in the previous books is completed in BOOK FOUR by introducing the idea for which the child is now prepared — sharing in the Divine Life.

The miracle which Jesus performed to prepare the minds of the people for the great miracle of the Holy Eucharist

Source Material for Book Four

is used, in story and test form, as an apperceptive basis to prepare the mind of the child to receive the doctrine of the Living Bread. The child is taught about the Living Bread, the promises connected with the Living Bread, and the fulfillment of these promises in the words of Consecration.

To strengthen faith in and devotion to the Holy Eucharist, use is made of the feast days and hymns in honor of the Blessed Sacrament, which have been the means of strengthening the faith of the people throughout the ages.

The teacher should call attention to other means which the Church has used to increase devotion to the Blessed Sacrament, such as processions, societies in honor of the Blessed Sacrament, and Eucharistic Congresses.

The value of fervent preparation for Holy Communion may well be stressed again and again. If the teacher thinks it advisable, the meaning and the effects of a sacrilege might be introduced in this discussion.

Although the child has been receiving Holy Communion for some time, it seems fitting in a lesson on the Holy Eucharist to review quite simply and thoroughly points which are helpful to the child as an immediate preparation for Holy Communion. It will help him to appreciate his great privilege in being allowed to receive Holy Communion every day if he knows about the restoration by Pope Pius X of the custom of receiving Holy Communion frequently and about his special desire to have children begin to receive Holy Communion while very young.

The following excerpt from the Summa gives the opinion of St. Thomas concerning daily Communion.

But this Sacrament is spiritual food; hence, just as bodily food is taken every day, so it is a good thing to receive this Sacrament every day. Hence it is that Our Lord (St. Luke 11 : 3) teaches us to pray : " Give us this day our daily bread."

A Topic on the Holy Eucharist would not be properly finished without an effort to stimulate a desire for adoration of the Blessed Sacrament.

Stories like those of Blessed Imelda, Peter Eymard, and St. Clare may be used for this purpose. The story of Tarcisius is given on page 141 of BOOK FOUR.

TOPIC NINETEEN : LIVING IN THE KING'S SERVICE

Topic Nineteen begins with the quotation, " Everyone hath his proper gift from God; one after this manner, and another after that," introducing the subject of vocations. The marriage vocation with its permanence, its responsibility, and its sanction by God is explained. Next the gift of virginity with its sanction by God and special prerogatives is explained. And then the priestly state is presented with its special powers and great dignity.

God's children should be taught to show gratitude to God for giving to His priests the power to administer the Sacraments, and also taught to show special respect toward priests and to pray for them.

The Sacrament of Extreme Unction is taught on page 154 under the heading " Dying in the King's Service." This Topic is introduced by the Bible verses from St. James (5 : 14, 15) and St. Mark (6 : 13). Then comes an explanation of the prayers said in the anointing. For it seems best that the child should be taught these beautiful prayers so that his first acquaintance with them will not be at a death-bed.

In this Topic the child learns all that it seems necessary for him to know in order to be properly prepared for the administration of the Sacrament of Extreme Unction.

It seems appropriate to introduce here the subject of sacramentals because so many sacramentals are used in the administration of this Sacrament.

Topic Twenty: Strength for the King's Service

The Sacrament of Confirmation is the subject matter of Topic Twenty. An appreciation of this Sacrament and a strengthening of the faith will result from an adequate and thorough presentation of what this Sacrament means and the effect it produces in the soul of the recipient.

The title of this Topic, " Strength for the King's Service," indicates to the child the nature of the effect produced through this stream of grace.

In order that this Topic may be approached with a good preparation, the apperceptive basis used is a discussion of different kinds of strength, leading up to the strength which the grace of Confirmation gives to the mind and will.

Under the headings " Champions of the Faith in the New-Born Church " and " The First Pentecost," the Biblical setting is given to the child, showing him graphically the effects of the tremendous power received through the first coming of the Holy Ghost. The child is led through early Church history to see the marvelous effects of the courage and strength which the early Christian martyrs received through the power of the Holy Ghost. Then he is taught that through the Sacrament of Confirmation spiritual maturity is attained, or in the words of St. Paul, "When I became a man, I put away the things of a child."

The meaning of this spiritual maturity is further developed in the child's mind through practical questions concerning fear. It would be well for the teacher to formulate other practical questions which have a direct bearing upon the home and school life of the group of children he is teaching.

The reason the Sacrament of Confirmation is called the Sacrament of the Holy Ghost is carefully developed through Bible texts, and on page 172 the historical development of the Sacrament of Confirmation is given.

A comparison of the effects of the grace received in the Sacraments of Baptism, Holy Eucharist, and Confirmation is made under the heading, "The Seed, the Nourishment, and the Strength of Grace."

The material used by the Church in the administration of the Sacraments always has a symbolic meaning. The symbolism of the materials used in Confirmation is taught on pages 175 and 176. The symbolism of what is done in Confirmation is also explained.

The child is told just what to do to prepare for the Sacrament of Confirmation. Practically all of the ceremony is given so that through a better understanding he will have a greater impetus for making a thorough preparation for the reception of the Sacrament.

An effort is made to inspire the child with the idea that through the Sacrament of Confirmation he is enrolled as a soldier of the King of Kings and is given great courage and strength to prove his love by enduring sufferings willingly in the cause of his King.

Source Material for Book Four

Under the heading "The King's Champion," the child is taught that just as natural cowardice is disgraceful in a soldier, so spiritual cowardice is disgraceful in one who is confirmed. Bible texts are given showing the punishment for disloyalty and the reward for loyalty in the King's service.

By means of the problems on page 184 the child is brought face to face with the type of spiritual battles he may be asked to fight every day to prove his loyalty. The teacher may use these problems as a basis for the formulation of other problems applicable to the children he is teaching.

In Topic Ten in BOOK THREE the child learned about the work attributed to each Person of the Blessed Trinity and a foundation was laid for an understanding of the work of the Holy Ghost dwelling within the soul and sanctifying it. Now in Topic Twenty, under the heading "The Divine Architect," the child is taught that the perfection of the image and likeness of God in the individual soul is the work of the Holy Ghost. He also learns that this image and likeness cannot reach perfection without individual suffering and that the strength to bear this suffering comes in a special way through the Sacrament of Confirmation.

The seven gifts of the Holy Ghost are correlated with the seven virtues — the three divine virtues and the four cardinal virtues — as perfecting and strengthening them. The gifts are taught as Fiery Spirits sent into the soul by the Holy Ghost and giving to the soul seven different powers and seven different helps to perfection.

In the series of tests on "What Gift and What Virtue?" a saint is pointed out as having illustrated a particular gift to a remarkable degree. The effects of the virtue and the gift on the child's own mind and will are also indicated.

After the gifts and virtues have been taught, the child is shown how the gifts oppose the seven deadly sins and conquer them, and in a test he is asked to tell the quality in the gift which conquers the sin.

The child learns the beatitudes as blessed results which follow the presence of the Fiery Spirits in the soul. If he understands correctly the beatitude and the corresponding gift, he can recognize the particular quality and the kind of action which would give evidence that the person possesses the beatitude.

In a test following the discussion of each beatitude, the child is asked to make a definite choice of qualities and actions to show the correctness of his knowledge of this beatitude. Many other tests on each beatitude and on several of them combined may be worked out by the teacher, using as models those given in the textbook.

Through study of the fact in nature that a fruit tree to fulfill its end must bear fruit, the child is led to understand the Scriptural injunction that we must bear spiritual fruit and that by the fruit the tree is known. Under the heading "I Must Bring Forth Fruit," the two parables of the fig tree and the Bible verses from St. John 15: 16 are used.

The teacher will note that the child is invited to think about what Our Lord's words mean. This plan lays a basis for meditation and is used throughout the study of the fruits.

In the discussion of the fruits of the Spirit, the comparison to a natural garden is sustained. The Holy Ghost is called the Master Gardener. The child is taught that the choicest fruit that the Master Gardener has in His garden is charity or love and that the other fruits come with the rivers of love from the Master's garden.

THE INTERPRETATION OF THE PICTURES

The design on the cover of each book gives the keynote to the doctrine presented in the book. The covers would therefore furnish excellent material for picture study after the proper apperceptive basis has been established.

BOOK ONE

THE COVER

The cover represents two children starting out on a journey. They are to travel along the Spiritual Way, where they will meet and see many wonderful things. An angel watches over them on their journey.

The lunette on page 1 of BOOK FOUR shows the same two children at the end of their quest.

In the border of the cover many children may be seen doing various things; all are traveling along the Spiritual Way.

THE FOREWORD

At the top of the page is a seal of the Religious of the Cenacle. The letters N.D.C. in the center mean *Nostra Domina a Cœnaculo*, the Latin words for Our Lady of the Cenacle. The dove is represented in this seal because it is a symbol of the Holy Ghost.

Around the oval is the Cenacle motto, taken from the Acts of the Apostles (1 : 14). "All these were persevering with one mind in prayer with . . . Mary, the mother of Jesus."

This motto describes a scene in the first Cenacle in Jerusalem after Our Lord had ascended into heaven. At the time of His Ascension He told His disciples to go into the city to pray until He would send the Holy Ghost upon them.

Topic One

The lunette on page 1 shows a little boy sitting upon a rock. He has just finished studying Topic One. What he has learned causes him to think deeply about the great truth: "The Lord he is God: he made us."

The pictures on pages 4, 5, 6, and 7 represent the creatures created by God on the different days of creation.

The beautifully illustrated poem on pages 18 and 19 may be used both as a memory exercise and as a picture lesson to enrich the study of Topic One. The child may be asked to enumerate the creatures of God shown in the picture.

Topic Two

The capital letter on page 24 gives the keynote both to the music and to the subject matter used as an application in Topic Two. The child will probably be interested if his attention is directed to this.

The teacher should be sure that the children know how to interpret correctly the pictures on pages 27, 28, and 41.

The picture on page 31 will associate the coming of the Light of Grace with Baptism. Both the pouring of the water and the coming of the Light are represented in the picture.

The three-paneled picture on page 43 shows children thinking of God at different times during the day: saying

Interpretation of the Pictures

grace before meals; saying a prayer as they pass a church; asking God's help during study. These pictures may be utilized by the teacher for study, and the children may be asked to suggest other times when they might want to think of God in a special way.

The picture on page 47 shows a prince carrying a shield and a banner. The motto on the banner is: "For love of the king; brave, kind, true." The lion in the picture symbolizes courage; the heart, love and kindness; the daisy in the lion's mouth, truth; and the crown symbolizes royalty. Those of royal blood inherited the privilege of having a crown upon their shields. But sometimes the king granted this privilege to one of his subjects as a special favor.

Topic Three

The lunette on page 55 should be studied after Topic Three has been taught, for it shows Noë and his three sons offering sacrifice. It would be well to have the children note the primitive altar. But as they have not yet studied sacrifices of the Old Law, their attention need not be called to the victim being burned.

They should notice the attitude of reverence shown by the four men and also the words printed in the lunette.

The children will surely be interested in the picture on page 57 showing Noë and his sons building the ark. They will also be interested in the border showing the animals that probably went into the ark. They will see that two of each kind are represented.

The picture on page 59 shows the king's servant dismissing Moses and Aaron outside the throne room. The oriental costumes and the expressive attitude of the characters should be noted.

The picture on page 65 represents Moses and some of God's people camped on the shores of the Red Sea. They suddenly see Pharao and his army in the distance following them.

Topic Four

It will prove interesting to the children to know that the eye surrounded by rays in the capital letter at the beginning of Topic Four (page 82) is a symbol representing the fact that God sees and knows all things. This should not be called to the child's attention until after the Topic has been taught, as it gives the keynote to the entire lesson.

The very beautiful border surrounding the Our Father on page 109 represents children of various nations saying this prayer to the One Who is Father of them all. In the lower panel a family is gathered in prayer saying the Our Father.

At the beginning of this book, the child learns that man is a creature of God. A little later he learns that he shares in something of God Himself, and for this reason is a child of God.

The child has been carefully led throughout the book to realize his duty and privileges as creature and child of God. In the last part of the book he is taught that he can render to God praise, honor, and thanksgiving through the most perfect of all prayers. He is left at the end with a beautiful illustration which conveys to him the message that this is the prayer for all times and all people.

BOOK TWO

The Cover

The two children who were represented on the cover of BOOK ONE as starting out on their journey along the Spiritual Way have now reached a place where they meet two horsemen. On the cover of BOOK TWO the horsemen are shown, but the children cannot be seen.

One of these men rides a white horse. He sits erect, looks straight ahead, and is calm and brave. The other man rides a black horse. He does not sit erect, looks down, and seems dejected and fearful. The indistinct picture of the horseman typifies the fact that he is living in darkness, having chosen to cut himself off from the Light of Grace.

The two inscriptions are like signposts. The Latin words *Vita Bonis* mean " Life to the Good," and *Mors est malis* means " Death to the wicked."

As the children study these inscriptions, they know from their lesson on " The Kingdom of Noblest Princes and Princesses " that the rider on the white horse is a noble and true prince following the road leading to his Father's kingdom. And they also know from this same lesson that the rider of the black horse has been foolish and untrue and that he is following the road leading away from Light into darkness.

Topic Five

The lunette on page 1 is the artist's way of representing the Particular Judgment.

The upper part of the picture shows three medallions.

The word "time" is in the one at the left; the word "death" in the center medallion; and three question marks are in the one at the right, which represents eternity. Question marks are used in this medallion because, for the soul departing, eternity may mean heaven or hell.

The clock in the picture shows twelve o'clock as the moment of death. This is the artist's way of showing that, for the soul leaving the body, time is no more.

The scale shown in the picture is the scale of justice. The fruit in the left scale-pan represents grace. The dark thorns in the right scale-pan represent the absence of grace. At the left of the picture is the guardian angel, and below is the sentence of the good, "Come ye blessed." On the other side appears a bad angel and the sentence of the wicked, "Depart ye cursed."

TOPIC SIX

The initial at the opening of Topic Six (page 22) has the cross, the heart, and the anchor within it — the symbols of faith, hope, and charity. After the children have been taught the Acts, it would add interest to call their attention to these symbols.

TOPIC SEVEN

In the initial letter on page 52 a crown is represented to suggest the underlying theme of the Topic, which is the kingdom of heaven. The panel following the discussion of heaven, page 55, is suggestive of peace, order, and beauty.

The decorative drawing on page 60 is a design suggesting one of the elements of hell — disorder and chaos.

The lunette on page 65 shows the unity of the Church on

Interpretation of the Pictures

earth, in purgatory, and in heaven. This unity is expressed by the term "the Communion of Saints." The shield, the helmet, and the sword are the armor of the Christian on earth (Ephesians 6:16, 17). The cross is the symbol of faith; the anchor, of hope; the heart, of love; and the palm and lily signify victory and purity.

Topic Eight

The closed gate in the initial letter at the beginning of Topic Eight (page 82) represents the closing of the gate of paradise after the sin of Adam and Eve.

The illustrations on pages 84 and 86 are companion pictures. The picture on page 84 represents the adopted prince before his fatal choice; the one on page 86 shows him after the choice. Attention should be called to the text in the picture on page 86 because the text applies with just as much truth to every man as it did to Adam. The panel on page 90, showing an ax and a hoe, is suggestive of the labors which Adam had to undergo in tilling the earth after he chose to turn against God.

In the picture on page 100 purity is suggested by the chasteness of the pillars and platform, together with the words printed across the top, "For the temple of God is holy." The dragon of impurity is attempting to enter the temple. The attitude of the boy and the thorny club he is wielding show that positiveness of will is necessary to overcome any exterior intrusion of an impure nature. It would seem that this strong picture could not help having a good psychological and moral effect upon the child. It should make a mental picture which would function as an armor in the hour of a child's temptation.

The Spiritual Way: Manual

Topic Nine

The decorative material in the capital (page 107) and illustrations of Topic Nine is suggestive of sin and suffering.

In the picture on page 125 showing the Ten Commandments, there are two figures at the bottom suggesting the cherubim, which God commanded to be made and placed at the corners of the ark of the covenant. In the center of the bottom panel is a representation of the tablets of stone which Moses received.

BOOK THREE

The Cover

The children traveling along the Spiritual Way now find the " Expected of the Ages " as a Babe in His Mother's arms.

The little lamb coming to the Baby in the picture symbolizes the truth that the sacrificial lambs of the Old Law were valuable only because they led to the Sacrifice of the one true Lamb in the New Law.

Topic Ten

The lunette giving the keynote to Topic Ten (page 1) represents two angels offering the incense of praise to God. The words of praise of the angelic chorus in honor of the Blessed Trinity are printed below.

The shamrocks in the initial letter on page 1 are suggestive of the doctrinal point which is treated in Topic Ten.

Topic Eleven

The picture on page 33 represents two pagans greeting the dawn which will dispel the darkness of unbelief. Around

Interpretation of the Pictures 83

them are broken idols. The words printed in the picture express the longing of their hearts.

The picture on page 35 shows a group of people afflicted in various ways waiting for the coming of Jesus. The I.H.S. at the left of the picture is an abbreviation of the Greek form of the name of Jesus — Iesous.

The mark at the middle of the right-hand panel is called the chirho. It consists of two letters, X and P, which make up the Greek form of the name of Christ. Titus III–IV, printed at the left of the arch near the top, tells us that the words at the bottom of the picture are taken from the Epistle of St. Paul to Titus, Chapter three, verse four.

On page 47 is a study picture to be used with the text on page 46. Each division of the picture represents an article of the Apostles' Creed.

The picture on page 49 represents the fourteen Stations of the Cross in simple form to be used as a study lesson in connection with the life of Jesus.

The picture on page 55 is a favorite design for the cover of the Gospels. In the corners are four winged creatures. In the upper left corner the angel with the human face represents St. Matthew, who begins his Gospel with the human ancestry of Our Lord. The lion represents St. Mark, for the lion lives in the desert, and St. Mark begins by telling of St. John the Baptist, who was " the voice of one crying in the wilderness." The ox represents St. Luke, for in his first chapter he speaks of the priest Zachary and the priests of the Old Testament who offered oxen in sacrifice. The eagle represents St. John, because the eagle soars high in the heavens and St. John speaks at once of the Divinity of Our Lord.

Topic Twelve

The initial letter on page 66 gives the keynote of the Topic. The Ave Maria, the Latin for " Hail Mary," and the white flowers symbolizing purity prepare the mind for the subject to be studied — Mary, Mother of Jesus.

The picture on page 73 will give the child who studies it a special realization of the beauty and purity which enshroud the mystery of the angel's visit to the Blessed Virgin Mary. Everything about the texture of the picture itself is in harmony with the mystery which it represents.

In the picture on page 83 wreaths of roses represent the Rosary; the joyful mysteries are indicated by the white roses; the sorrowful mysteries by the orange roses; and the glorious mysteries by the pale orange roses.

Topic Thirteen

It will be very interesting for the child to study the picture on page 97 showing the primitive offering of the sacrifices of the Old Law and to select the gifts that the people are bringing to offer in sacrifice.

Topic Fourteen

The picture on page 128 containing the prophecy of Malachias is an interesting study. The grapes and wheat symbolize the bread and wine of the sacrifice. The panels at the sides show northern and southern scenes; the upper and lower panels represent oriental and western civilization. The picture as a whole is designed to tell of the offering of the Holy Sacrifice of the Mass from the rising to the setting of the sun, which means that there is no time of the twenty-

Interpretation of the Pictures 85

four hours when Holy Mass is not being offered in some part of the world, fulfilling the prophecy of Malachias.

Compare the lamb in the background of the picture on page 135 with the lamb in the picture on page 105 and with the one in the upper left-hand corner of page 149.

The lamb is the symbol of Christ. From the fifth century artists pictured its head as encircled with the nimbus or halo as shown on page 135. About a century later they began the custom of picturing the lamb with its side pierced and its blood flowing into a chalice, as you can see in the picture on page 149.

According to Scripture, God is the Source of Light; and so a halo of light is an appropriate symbol. As saints are children of the Light, they are honored by a halo to show that they are sharers in the Light. The halo of a saint is either a plain circle 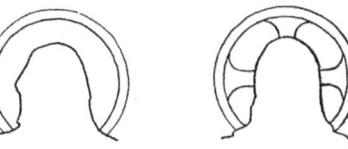 (diagram 1) or an ornamented circle whereas that of the deity is usually the cruciform nimbus or circle containing a cross (diagram 2).

Throughout the border of the picture on page 149, the wheat and grapes symbolize the bread and wine used in the Mass. The pelican in the upper right-hand corner is a bird which is supposed to feed its young with its own blood; so it is used as an emblem of Our Lord. The symbol of the lamb with its blood flowing into the chalice is used in the upper left corner. Jesus and His eleven faithful Apostles express the main thought of this picture.

BOOK FOUR

THE COVER

The design on the cover of BOOK FOUR represents the seven Sacraments. In the center is a picture of an ostensorium containing the Holy Eucharist. On either side are six angels holding symbols of the other Sacraments. They are from left to right: Matrimony, symbolized by two rings; Confirmation by a dove; Baptism by a baptismal shell; Holy Orders by a stole and the book of Gospels; Penance by keys; and Extreme Unction by a crucifix and oil-stock.

The rays are symbolic of the grace which is received through the Sacraments. The seven lighted candles express the living faith and love of all those who believe in the Divine Presence in the Holy Eucharist.

TOPIC FIFTEEN

The lunette on page 1 introducing BOOK FOUR pictures children and grown-up people of many nations, suggesting the universality or catholicity of the Church.

The boy and girl who were pictured on the cover of BOOK ONE as starting along the Spiritual Way appear in this lunette as having found "a path and a way . . . called the holy way." For when the prophet Isaias spoke the words written at the bottom of the lunette, he foretold the true Spiritual Way through which we may grow in grace and holiness.

The bishop and the priest are shown in the picture welcoming the little ones.

Interpretation of the Pictures

The tall pointed cap which the bishop is wearing is called a *mitre* and it is a sign of episcopal authority.

The pastoral staff which the bishop holds is called a *crosier* and typifies his duties as shepherd of the flock.

The priest wears a *stole* around his neck. The stole is the specific mark of the priestly office, being the badge of deaconal and priestly authority.

The picture on page 5 representing Our Lord sending the Apostles to convert the world will be an interesting study for children because of the grouping and the attitudes of the Apostles.

The beautifully decorated text on page 13 contains the commission of Our Lord to St. Peter, "Feed my lambs, feed my sheep." It is rich in symbolism.

In the upper panel Jesus is pictured as the Good Shepherd with His sheep. The boys and girls in the lower panel represent the lambs of the Good Shepherd's fold.

In the upper corners are crosses, and in the lower corners are inverted crosses with **P** in the center. These inverted crosses symbolize the fact that St. Peter was crucified with head downward.

St. Peter is represented in the panel on the left and Pope Pius XI, one of his successors, in the panel on the right. In the panel with the head of St. Peter we see the crosier of a bishop, for the Pope is the Bishop of Rome. In the panel on the right is shown the processional cross with treble traverse. The treble traverse is used only on the processional cross of the Pope.

In the picture on page 25 the vine symbolizes Jesus; the branches, those who have the Light of Grace shining in their souls.

The picture on page 37 represents St. Peter as the rock on which the Church is built. The words which Jesus used when He gave Peter the keys and the power to bind and loose are printed in the middle of the picture. At the top of the picture are shown the keys and the tiara. At the bottom St. Peter himself is represented in an attitude of deep humility. The pillars on the sides represent the Church.

TOPIC SIXTEEN

The fountain on page 47 surmounted by the cross symbolizes Jesus' Church. Jesus is the Source of grace, and the grace coming from Jesus to His Church is symbolized in the picture by the main stream coming from the base of the cross. The seven smaller streams coming from the main stream symbolize the seven Sacraments. On the scroll is written an Act of Faith in the One, Holy, Catholic, and Apostolic Church. For the Latin phrase means " And in One Holy Catholic and Apostolic Church: I believe."

The picture on page 54 will be a help to the children in studying the Baptism of blood. The girl bound for martyrdom is looking with firm faith into eternity. In the background is the cross, a symbol of the Source from which this girl receives the strength to face suffering so courageously. The palm leaf symbolizes victory. The cross and crown symbolize her death and entrance into heaven.

TOPIC SEVENTEEN

The panel on page 81 contains the words spoken by Jesus at the time He gave the power to forgive sin. The Holy Spirit is represented by the dove at the top of the panel.

Interpretation of the Pictures

On the right and left are the cross, the keys, and the stole. The cross symbolizes Jesus; the keys, the power to bind and loose; and the stole, the authority given by Jesus to His priests.

TOPIC TWENTY

The picture on page 165 represents the descent of the Holy Ghost in the form of tongues of fire upon the Blessed Virgin Mary and the disciples. The history of this event is told in the Acts of the Apostles.

The flowers in the initial on page 214, which opens the discussion of spiritual fruits, are symbolic. The lily symbolizes purity, and the rose, love and beauty.

The Spiritual Way series closes with a decorative text of the Veni Creator Spiritus. In the border at the top of the picture the Holy Spirit is represented by a dove surrounded by tongues of fire with rays going forth from them. Arranged around the border in circles of flowers, the names of the fruits of the Holy Spirit are written in Latin. In the left border are charity, patience, benignity, longanimity, faith, and continency. In the right border are peace, joy, goodness, mildness, modesty, and chastity. Flowers of many varieties are in the border. At the bottom of the picture a group of children are singing this hymn to the Holy Ghost.

PROJECTS

The life of every normal child is active. In his activity he is continually working out problems and carrying out projects of his own. As he lives, he learns to think, because in his effort to carry out a definite purpose he meets difficulties and thinks out a way of overcoming them.

The teacher should remember this normal process of development and plan his Christian Doctrine lessons so that the child will have the right kind of problems to solve and projects to carry out. This is in a true sense what some modern educators call purposeful activity.

Problems and projects used in this way are based upon sound psychology because they are based upon sound reasoning processes. Therefore, they emphasize reasoning rather than mere memorizing.

Throughout *The Spiritual Way* problems are given which are based on sound doctrinal points and which touch the practical life of the child, both now and in the future. This is purposeful activity in its broad sense, because it enters not only into the individual life of the child but also into the school and home life. If the child becomes interested enough to carry out projects of his own, this activity will develop his spiritual life and reach out into the life of his family and even of the community.

The more worth-while problems a child solves and the more worth-while projects he carries out, the more practical will his spirituality be for himself and for others.

One project is carried throughout *The Spiritual Way* series. This is the making of an individual Catechism book, called a Project Book, although any other suitable name might be selected. Directions for making this book are given on pages 7 and 8 of BOOK ONE.

The Project Book fulfills several purposes: it is an avenue for the child's activity; he clarifies his ideas by expressing them in written form; the consciousness of having made his own Catechism gives the child a deeper interest in the subject; the parents' interest in the religious development of the child is secured and maintained.

As each Project Book represents a year's work, the teacher should have a regular plan for examining it and a growing list of the points to be noted for approval or disapproval. Some of these points would be correct doctrine, the use of headings, correct sentences, neatness, and general arrangement.

Throughout the four Project Books, the main point to be considered for criticism is correctness of doctrine. It is very important that this be carefully noted.

As the children progress from grade to grade, the standard for the examination of the other points should be gradually raised.

It is hoped that there will be a close coördination between the accuracy of the child's knowledge and his growth in power of correct expression.

If the child is stimulated to take a real interest in the making of a beautiful and correct set of Project Books, the result will be permanent interest and real creative thinking concerning the application of Christian Doctrine principles.

The making of an art collection is a valuable project. It may be either a part of the Project Book or a separate art book.

BOOK ONE

Topic One. In connection with Topic One, a project on the days of creation might be worked out. A large circle of green cartridge paper might be cut to represent the world. Then for each day of creation the child might cut out and paste pictures of the various creatures created on that day.

The work of creation as listed in Knecht's *Commentary on Holy Scripture* is as follows:

First day: The light ("divide the light from darkness")
Second day: The atmosphere which divides the waters
Third day: The dry land
Fourth day: The bodies of light — sun, moon, and stars
Fifth day: The inhabitants of the dry land — the beasts and man

White paper may be used for light; black for darkness; pale blue for the atmosphere; deep blue for the water; brown for the land; orange for the sun; yellow for the moon and stars. Pictures of birds, fish, beasts, and men may be cut from discarded magazine advertising material, or the teacher may draw models and have the children trace them. If preferred, boxes of bird, fish, and animal pictures can be secured.

Topic Two. During the study of Topic Two, the teacher may draw a model shield and have each child cut his own shield out of oak-tag or cardboard. In the history of heraldry, we ordinarily find the coat-of-arms on the shield.

The teacher may encourage the children to acts of courage, kindness, and truth by giving different colored stars for definite acts of these virtues. Let each child at the end of a certain period arrange his stars to form his coat-of-arms. Rubber stamp stars may be used with various colored inks.

Topic Three. For Topic Three the children might make a Praise Booklet, or they might draw various pictures showing creatures of God giving praise to Him. Pictures of birds singing, a church organist and choir, children singing, monks praying or singing, a beautiful sunset, a beautiful garden of flowers, would be appropriate. Under these various pictures, the children might write a statement telling how praise is being given to God.

Topic Four. This topic suggests the making of a booklet called "The Light of God." On the cover the children might paste a golden circle with rays of golden light coming from it. On the first inside page they might print "God Sees All Things." Under this could be drawn the eye of God as shown in the initial letter on page 82. Then the four headings, Cheerfulness, Good-temper, Truth and Honor, and Unselfishness might be used, dividing the pages into four parts. If the teacher provides a supply of stars of four different colors, they may be given to the children upon their own request when they wish to record their special acts under the different headings. After the child has a record of a definite number of acts of each type, the booklet should be handed to the teacher, who on returning it may give the child some token of approval.

The making of these acts would be a basis for the development of a sound interior life for the child.

BOOK TWO

Topic Five. The text on page 16 teaches that many holy people in all times have been willing to risk the health and beauty of their bodies to bring the Light of Grace into other souls and to increase it in their own. This reference may suggest to the children the making of a book for a given month entitled "A Saint for Each Day." The cover might be made of an attractive color and might have a picture pasted on it and be decorated according to the child's ability.

Each page might be devoted to some saint of the child's choice, with a picture where it is possible to secure it, a quotation from the saint's sayings, and an account of some action of the saint.

Where the teacher finds it practical, a project may be developed in connection with the reference on page 17 by having a particular altar decorated for a certain period of time.

The children may also be encouraged to collect from magazines and other sources pictures of beautiful cathedrals or altars for their art collection.

Topic Six. The keeping of a class aspiration chart is a project to enrich this Topic.

Two charts are necessary. On one of these are printed ten or more aspirations which would be desirable for the children to learn as a means of developing their spiritual life; on the other chart the children's names are printed. When an aspiration has been learned and said daily for a week by a child, a colored star might be placed after his name.

Another suggestion for a project would be to teach the children to make a spiritual bouquet consisting of Acts of Faith, Hope, and Love as a gift to their parents. They may make a cross for the symbol of faith, a heart for the symbol of love, and an anchor for the symbol of hope. These symbols are shown in the capital letter on page 22. The cross, heart, and anchor may be cut from gold or silver paper folded double. The number of Acts of Faith, Hope, and Love that the child has said may be written on the inside of the folded paper which symbolizes the Act.

Topic Seven. A project idea based upon the doctrine of the Communion of Saints could be developed by the use of a set of liturgical cards for the feast days of the year cut of uniform size. Then using the *Missal* or *The Liturgical Year* by Dom Gueranger, the children could be asked to find the name of the saint whose feast is being celebrated on that day. They could also be given, either orally or in written form, several statements concerning the life of the saint. The chief virtues of the saint could be discussed and the child asked to write several ways in which this virtue can be practiced in his own life. Where it is at all possible, a picture or something representing the saint should be pasted on the card.

Topic Eight. A very practical project for Topic Eight would be the establishment of the Angelic Warfare in the class. Pope Pius XI strongly urges its establishment in all institutions of education. For information, address The Angelic Warfare, 839 Lexington Avenue, New York City.

Topic Nine. The child might very well be introduced here to the practice of careful daily self-examination on the ordinary faults of his life, a practice advocated by many spiritual writers. The first step in carrying out this project is the making of a book, each page to be used for a series of ten questions with seven columns for the days of the week after each question. The child is to indicate his score with either a zero or a ten and at the bottom mark his final score for the day.

The teacher should stimulate the desire for growth from day to day.

The questions below are suggestive. The score is indicated in the Sunday column to show the way the child makes the record. After this set of questions has been used for a period of time long enough to show real development, other questions should be used.

A DAY OF VICTORIES

Keep your score in figures.
Count 10 each if you can answer *Yes*.

	S	M	T	W	T	F	S
1. Did I get up as soon as I was called?	0						
2. Did I say Good Morning to God by saying my prayers?	10						
3. Did I eat my meals without finding fault?	10						
4. Did I reach school at the right time?	0						
5. Did I deserve an A in conduct for the day?	0						
6. Did I do my work without cheating?	10						
7. Was I entirely truthful at home and at school?	10						
8. Was I a good sport at play, or was I angry when the game went against me?	10						
9. Did I do a kind deed for someone without expecting a reward?	10						
10. Can I count this day one in which I did not need to be ashamed of myself?	10						

Score 70

BOOK THREE

Topic Ten. The children are introduced here to the practice of keeping graphs of their test scores. The model is given on page 8. They are expected to keep graphs for the rest of the course.

In connection with the reading projects on page 23, the teacher might add the keeping of a book entitled " An Outline of the Spiritual Books I Have Read." The outline might include the following points:

1. Title
2. Author's name and a statement about the author
3. What the book is about
4. What part of the book the student likes best and the reason he likes it
5. Something in the book the student would like to remember

Another project would be organizing a day of retreat.

Topic Eleven. In connection with Topic Eleven the children might construct an art calendar, choosing pictures from the life of Our Lord.

The making of a Christmas crib and the staging of a nativity play or other plays are familiar projects.

The making of a booklet of the Stations of the Cross, either by drawing the pictures given on page 49 or by cutting out pictures and pasting them on separate pages, is an instructive and devotional project. Then prayers applicable to each Station are to be written below the pictures.

Another project is the organization of a Christian Doctrine club, having its own constitution and by-laws, president and other officers. Programs of various kinds concerning Christian Doctrine can be presented, such as dramatizations, dialogues, articles to be read, poems, liturgical practices, and notes on the lives of saints. Slides and moving pictures may be presented and speakers invited.

Topics Twelve, Thirteen, Fourteen. The projects developed in these Topics are clearly described in the book so that no further explanation is needed here. The teacher will probably find the projects in the textbook adequate for arousing the children's interest.

BOOK FOUR

The practice of keeping graphs introduced in BOOK THREE should be continued throughout BOOK FOUR. The model graph is given on page 7.

Throughout the study of this book a good project is the keeping of a record of symbolism in a section of the Project Book. Wherever possible, the children might draw the symbols and tell what they express. The study of symbolism for this project would be of three types:

1. The symbolism of the pictures in the textbook
2. The symbolic meaning of expressions in the text
3. The symbolism used in the ornamentation of churches

The symbolism of the pictures in the textbook is explained on pages 75–89 of this Manual.

There is a wealth of symbolism also in the text itself.

Page 1. The words at the bottom of the lunette are a symbolic prophecy concerning the Church from the Book of Isaias, in which he predicts that a path and a holy way will be given.

Page 8. In the Bible text given here, Jesus calls Peter the rock upon which He will build His Church. The rock is a symbol of strength. The kind of strength symbolized in this text is the strength of faith. Keys are used to lock and unlock doors. In this Bible text they are symbolic of the power which Jesus gave to Peter to forgive sins, thus enabling him to open heaven to sinners who are sorry for their sins. (See pages 79 and 111 in the textbook.)

Page 12. Jesus called Himself the Good Shepherd. Peter and his successors represent Jesus; each in turn is called the Good Shepherd on earth. Lambs and sheep symbolize people.

Page 28. The Mystical Body of Christ symbolizes the Church. Jesus is the Head of the Mystical Body and all people in the state of grace are its members.

Page 30. The corner-stone symbolizes Jesus. Living stones symbolize those in the state of grace.

Page 46. The fountain symbolizes the Church. The water of life symbolizes grace.

Page 64. Breathing upon the one to be baptized symbolizes the infusion of the Spirit of God. Making the Sign of the Cross upon the forehead and breast of a person signifies that he must be sanctified in mind and heart. The laying of the end of the stole on the one being baptized symbolizes admitting him into the body of the Church. When the priest changes the violet stole to the white one, it symbolizes the coming of grace. The lighted candle symbolizes the light of faith and the flame of charity.

Page 135. Spiritual flowers symbolize prayers and spiritual acts.

Page 164. The tongues of fire symbolize the coming of the Holy Ghost, the Spirit of Love.

Page 173. The incorruptible seed symbolizes grace.

Page 216. "Spiritual fruits" signifies the virtues.

ADDITIONAL TESTS AND PROBLEMS
BOOK ONE

Page 15. St. Thérèse of the Child Jesus

To be used as an application of "I belong to God" on page 15. After the story has been told to the children, they may write it in their Project Books and retell it orally.

St. Thérèse of the Child Jesus understood very well, even from the time she was a tiny girl, that she belonged to God. She tells us this in her story of her life in these words, "From the age of three I never refused the good God anything."

When she was older and found some things very hard to bear, knowing that she belonged to God, she used to think of herself as the little top of the Child Jesus. She tried to be the kind of top that He would like to play with and could spin a whole day without stopping. Because she thought of herself as a little top belonging to Jesus, she only smiled at the hard things she had to bear.

Page 15. A Test: Because I Belong to God

Fill in the blanks below and make complete sentences by beginning each one with *Because I Belong to God*. Copy the completed sentences in your Project Book.

I will serve God Who —— me.

B irds, flowers, and all other —— were made for me.
E verything I have is my —— gift to me.
L earning about —— is my duty.
O thers should —— about God through me.
N o —— can keep me from praising Him.
G od wants —— to praise Him.

T he ——, I will pray to Him every morning and evening.
O bedience is necessary for me as a —— of God.

Additional Tests and Problems

G od wants me to live for ——.
O thers should receive happiness through ——.
D o I have a right to forget ——?

The words for the blank spaces:

I	created	T	Creator
		O	creature
B	creatures		
E	Creator's	G	Him
L	God	O	me
O	learn	D	Him *or* God
N	creature *or* person		
G	me		

Pages 22 and 23. A Test: The Bible Verses and Music

Each question in Group II has an answer in Group I. Match the questions and answers correctly and write them in your Project Book.
Then ask your teacher if you have matched questions and answers correctly.

Group I

eight	shepherd
Gregorian Chant	St. Gregory
Psalm 99, verse 3	God
King David	all people
first tone	to give praise to God

Group II

1. Who wrote the Bible verses on page 23?
2. What was David's work before God called him to be king?
3. Why did David write these Bible verses?
4. Whom did David think of as Good Shepherd?
5. Whom did David think of as sheep of God's pasture?

The Spiritual Way: Manual

6. To what kind of music are the words "Know ye that the Lord he is God" set?
7. Who arranged this kind of music?
8. How many different tones of Gregorian Chant are there?
9. Which of these tones is used in the music of this lesson?
10. From what Psalm and verse are the words "Know ye that the Lord he is God" taken?

The correct answers:

Group II		Group I
1	is answered by	King David
2	is answered by	shepherd
3	is answered by	to give praise to God
4	is answered by	God
5	is answered by	all people
6	is answered by	Gregorian Chant
7	is answered by	St. Gregory
8	is answered by	eight
9	is answered by	first tone
10	is answered by	Psalm 99, verse 3

Page 41. A Test: God's Light and Beauty

Each question in Group II has an answer in Group I. Match the questions and answers correctly and write them in your Project Book.

Group I

the Light of Grace
the gift of sharing in God's Light and Beauty
at Baptism
God loves me tenderly
God, the Father of Lights
sanctifying grace
the power to know and love God Himself

Additional Tests and Problems

Group II

1. Who lets you share in His Own Light and Beauty?
2. What power do you have because God's Light is in you?
3. What does St. Thomas call the gift of sharing in God's Own Light and Beauty?
4. What does your Catechism call the gift of sharing in God's Own Light and Beauty?
5. When are you called out of darkness into God's Light?
6. What gift makes you God's child?
7. When the Light of Grace is in your soul, Who loves you as tenderly as a father?

The correct answers:

Group II		Group I
1	is answered by	God, the Father of Lights
2	is answered by	the power to know and love God Himself
3	is answered by	the Light of Grace
4	is answered by	sanctifying grace
5	is answered by	at Baptism
6	is answered by	the gift of sharing in God's Light and Beauty
7	is answered by	God loves me tenderly

Page 50. Additional Problems

1. Charles made a hard snowball. He threw the ball at Paul. Paul dodged. The ball hit an old man who was carrying bundles of groceries. The bundles were broken and the groceries were spilled in the street. Charles did not help pick up the groceries. He ran away.

2. Edna did not like her new hat. Her mother told her that

she could not afford to buy another hat. Edna tore the rim entirely off her hat. She told her mother that a bad boy had done this. Her mother was obliged to wear her own old hat all summer so that she could buy Edna another one.

3. Gertrude, Helen, and Florence lived in the same block and usually went home from school together. One afternoon Gertrude and Helen wanted to go to another girl's house to play, but they knew that their mothers would not want them to do this. They were afraid Florence would tell the truth. So they hid her hat and caused Florence to spend a half hour looking for it.

Page 76. Some Saints Who Spread God's Kingdom

These short accounts of a few of the Apostles of the Nations might be used as part of a missionary program during one class period. One child may give each account. Later the accounts may be used as Project Book exercises.

St. Patrick

St. Patrick, the great Apostle of Ireland, lived between the years 400 and 500. He converted the people living in Ireland to the Christian faith. The people of Ireland loved St. Patrick because he taught them about the true God. It is now more than fifteen hundred years since St. Patrick converted the people of Ireland, but they still love him and still believe in the faith which he taught them.

St. Augustine

St. Augustine was sent by Pope St. Gregory the Great to convert the people of England between the years 500 and 600. He converted the king and many of the people. This St. Augustine is not the Doctor of the Church, the son of St. Monica, who lived about one hundred years earlier.

Additional Tests and Problems

St. Boniface

St. Boniface, who lived between the years 700 and 800, is called the Apostle of Germany because he converted so many pagans to the true faith. St. Boniface and fifty-two companions were martyred because they were trying to convert the people.

St. Francis Xavier

St. Francis Xavier offered his life to God in the Society of Jesus. He lived at the time of St. Ignatius, the founder of that Society. This was between the years 1500 and 1600. He was sent to convert the people living in the Indies and Japan. He wanted to convert the people of China also, but he died before he had time to do this.

Because St. Francis Xavier converted so many people, he is the patron of all Catholic missions.

Page 101. A Problem Test: Forgiveness

In your Project Book make two columns like this:

COLUMN A	COLUMN B
He forgave trespasses against him.	He did not forgive trespasses against him.

Read each of the following sentences. If the sentence tells that a trespass was forgiven, put the number of the sentence in column A. If it tells that a trespass was *not* forgiven, put the number in column B.

1. Mabel took Eleanor's umbrella one rainy day. Eleanor walked home in the rain and because of this she became sick. When Mabel realized the injury she had done to Eleanor, she was ashamed. She brought the umbrella to Eleanor's house and also used some of the money in her bank to buy beautiful flowers. Eleanor accepted the flowers and invited Mabel to play with her.

2. Frank sat behind Matthew in school. Both boys were writing in their Project Books. The teacher had promised a prize for the neatest and best looking book. Matthew wrote well and kept his book neat and orderly. Frank did not want Matthew to get the prize, so all during the period he poked Matthew and kept shaking the desk.

The prize was given to Frank. He knew that he had spoiled Matthew's work and he felt very sorry. He gave the prize back to the teacher, telling the truth about what he had done. The teacher then gave the prize to Matthew. Matthew took the prize, but he would not speak to Frank.

3. John spilled a bottle of ink on the floor of the classroom. When the teacher asked who had spilled the ink, John said that William had done it. The teacher believed what John said and told William to sandpaper the floor until no ink spot could be seen. All during the recess time William had to sandpaper the floor, but there was still much ink on the floor. The teacher said that he must remain after school until the task was finished. Then John began to feel sorry and ashamed of his lie. He told the teacher that he, not William, had spilled the ink and that he would finish the scraping. William insisted on remaining to help John.

Answers: Column A: 1, 3   Column B: 2

Page 103. A Problem Test: Temptation

In your Project Book make two columns like this:

COLUMN A	COLUMN B
The temptation was fought	*The temptation was not fought*

Read each of the following sentences. If the sentence tells that the temptation was fought, put the number of the sentence in column A. If it tells that the temptation was *not* fought, put the number in column B.

Additional Tests and Problems

1. Mary tore the pages of her book. When her teacher asked about it, Mary said that she did not tear them.
2. John owed Frank ten cents. John put the money in an envelope on Frank's desk. Arthur wanted the money. He took it.
3. Helen gave up candy during Lent. Rose offered her some candy at recess. Helen never wanted candy so much. She refused the candy.
4. Paul's father told him not to try to swim across a certain lake. The boys dared Paul to do this. Paul did not have the courage to stand the boys' jeering. He disobeyed his father.
5. William's mother told him to come directly home from school. The boys with whom William generally played needed one more boy for the baseball nine. They teased William to stay and play. William stayed.

Answers: Column A: 3   Column B: 1, 2, 4, 5

BOOK TWO

Page 19. Additional Problems

1. Alice did not like Susan. She did not bow to Susan when she met her.
2. John was supposed to serve at seven o'clock Mass. John was awake but he did not get up in time to serve.
3. It was Parents' Day at school. Helen's mother came to see the beautiful work that Helen had done. Some of the girls noticed that Helen's mother had on the same dress she had worn the year before. But Helen did not care about this. She acted in a way that showed much affection for her mother.
4. William was given some candy at a school party. He brought half of his candy home to his little brother.

Answers: Column A: 3, 4   Column B: 1, 2

Page 47. A Test: Making Acts of Faith, Hope, and Charity

Each question in Group II has an answer in Group I. Match the questions and answers correctly and write them in your Project Book.

Group I

a. that we believe in Him
b. an Act of Hope
c. to love Him daily more and more
d. worship God by faith, hope, and charity
e. every day
f. strengthen our faith
g. to believe in Him, hope in Him, and to love Him

Group II

1. What must we do to save our souls?
2. How does God want you to use your mind and your will?
3. When we make an Act of Faith, what do we tell God?
4. When we make an Act of Faith, what do we ask God to do for us?
5. When we tell God that we are sure He will make all our hopes come true, what Act is this?
6. When we make an Act of Love, what do we ask God to teach us?
7. How often should we make Acts of Faith, Hope, and Love?

The correct answers:

Group II		Group I
1	is answered by	d
2	is answered by	g
3	is answered by	a
4	is answered by	f
5	is answered by	b
6	is answered by	c
7	is answered by	e

Additional Tests and Problems

Page 63. A Test: The Particular Judgment

Copy Groups I and II in your Project Book. Read the first statement in Group I. Then find the statement in Group II which explains it. Put the number of the explanation in the parenthesis before the statement in Group I. Do the same with the other statements and explanations.

Group I: Statements

( ) When the soul leaves your body, it will then know whether it is to be in heaven, hell, or purgatory.

( ) Each soul is judged as soon as it leaves the body.

( ) At the Particular Judgment, if God's image and likeness in your soul are as clear and perfect as God wants them to be, great happiness will be yours.

( ) At the Particular Judgment, if there is none of God's Light and Beauty in your soul, great unhappiness will be yours forever.

( ) At the Particular Judgment, if the Light of Grace is in the soul but God's image and likeness are not as clear and perfect as God wants them to be, this soul must wait and suffer for a time.

Group II: Explanations

1. At the Particular Judgment, if God's image and likeness in a soul are as clear and perfect as God wants them to be, that soul will be in heaven forever.

2. The state of waiting and suffering after death until the soul is ready to be with God in heaven is called purgatory.

3. Immediately after death the soul is judged.

4. At the Particular Judgment, if there is none of God's Light and Beauty in a soul, it must be in hell forever.

5. The judgment which takes place immediately after death is called the Particular Judgment.

110 The Spiritual Way: Manual

The correct answers:

Group I		Group II
1	is explained by	3
2	is explained by	5
3	is explained by	1
4	is explained by	4
5	is explained by	2

Page 77. True and False Test: The Fourth and Fifth Commandments

On a page of your Project Book make two columns. Head the first column *True* and the second column *False*.

Read each of the following sentences. If the sentence is true, put the number of the sentence in the column marked *True*. If it is not true, put the number in the *False* column.

1. It was a rule of the school that no one should run down the stairs. Charles ran down the stairs. He kept the fourth Commandment.

2. Beatrice lost her temper and spoke in an angry and disagreeable way to Loretta. Beatrice broke the fifth Commandment.

3. The pastor told all the boys of Anthony's age to come to the church for instructions at a certain time. Anthony did not come, although he could easily have done so. He kept the fourth Commandment.

4. All the children in a certain class knew that when they passed through the hall for recess they were to keep to the right. Paul purposely walked to the left. Paul broke the fourth Commandment.

5. Several girls were playing tag. Nora purposely pushed Catherine so hard that Catherine fell and hurt herself. Nora kept the fifth Commandment.

The true sentences: 2, 4
The false sentences: 1, 3, 5

Additional Tests and Problems

Page 121. A Test: The Seventh and Eighth Commandments

Copy Groups I and II in your Project Book.
Read the first statement in Group I. Then find the statement in Group II which explains it. Put the number of the explanation in the parenthesis before the statement in Group I. Do the same with the other statements and explanations.

Group I: Statements

( ) John found a watch. He did not try to find the owner. He broke the seventh Commandment.

( ) Peter lived in the city. He drove into the country in an automobile with some friends. He and his friends took a bag of apples from an orchard without asking the owner. Peter and those with him broke the seventh Commandment.

( ) Julia found a ring at school. She knew that it belonged to Kate. She liked the ring and did not return it. She must return it before she will be forgiven.

( ) Maria's mother told her not to pick the flowers in the garden. When her mother washed Maria's dress, she found a flower in the pocket. She asked Maria about it. Maria said that the wind blew the flower into her pocket. Maria broke the eighth Commandment.

( ) Henry thought that it would be fun to cut the tire of an automobile parked in front of the school. He did it. Henry broke the seventh Commandment.

( ) Jennie did not do her homework in arithmetic because she went to a party. She knew that Agnes came to school early and nearly always had a perfect paper in arithmetic. Jennie went to school early and took Agnes's homework from her desk when Agnes went out of the room. Jennie copied the homework and tore up Agnes's paper. Agnes was marked *failure* and Jennie *perfect*. Jennie broke the eighth Commandment by accepting the mark given her.

The Spiritual Way: Manual

Group II: Explanations

1. Anyone who steals anything must, as far as he is able, return it or its value, before he will be forgiven.
2. Any willful injury done to another's property breaks the law of justice and is a sin against the seventh Commandment.
3. When anyone finds money or other valuables, in order to keep the seventh Commandment, he must try to find the owner.
4. Acting a lie is a sin against the eighth Commandment.
5. Taking and keeping even small amounts to which we have no right is stealing.
6. Anyone who tells a lie of any kind breaks the eighth Commandment.

The correct answers:

Group I		Group II
1	is explained by	3
2	is explained by	5
3	is explained by	1
4	is explained by	6
5	is explained by	2
6	is explained by	4

Page 122. A Test: The Ninth and Tenth Commandments

Copy Groups I and II in your Project Book.

Read the first statement in Group I. Then find the statement in Group II which explains it. Put the number of the explanation in the parenthesis before the statements in Group I. Do the same with the other statements and explanations.

Group I: Statements

( ) Several girls were telling stories. One girl started to tell an impure story. Gertrude immediately said, "I will not listen to this story." The girl did not stop, so Gertrude went away. Gertrude kept the ninth Commandment.

( ) Harry wrote an impure note. He broke the ninth Commandment.

( ) Michael drew an impure picture. He broke the ninth Commandment.

( ) John was at a moving picture. One act caused an impure thought to come into his mind. John broke the ninth Commandment.

( ) Pearl had a new pair of roller skates. When Kate saw the skates, she wanted them so much that she would have taken them, but others were looking. Pearl broke the tenth Commandment.

GROUP II: EXPLANATIONS

1. Looking at impure pictures causes impure thoughts to come into the mind.

2. We are commanded by the ninth Commandment to keep ourselves pure in thought.

3. Drawing impure pictures shows that impure thoughts are in the mind.

4. The tenth Commandment forbids all desires to take or keep wrongfully what belongs to another.

5. Writing an impure note shows that impure thoughts are in the mind.

The correct answers:

GROUP I		GROUP II
1	is explained by	2
2	is explained by	5
3	is explained by	3
4	is explained by	1
5	is explained by	4

ANSWERS TO THE TESTS

The tests used in *The Spiritual Way* series are much more than checking-up or drill exercises. They are introduced throughout the Topics as real purposeful activities, to stimulate interest, to develop power of concentration, and to test knowledge of doctrinal truth by presenting it under another aspect and often with additional Biblical material and from another point of view.

The tests may be used as an oral exercise conducted by the teacher or they may form the basis of a socialized recitation, with a child who has mastered the test presiding. Finally the tests should be used as written exercises and the individual child should be required to master each test.

BOOK ONE

Page 13. Right and Wrong Test

Sentences that are not true: 1, 4, 6, 7, 10, 11
Untrue sentences changed to tell the truth:
1. I cannot make things out of nothing.
4. Horses are not chief creatures of God.
6. God is not a creature.
7. My mother made a cake.
10. We cannot see angels because they have no bodies.
11. All creatures cannot work problems in arithmetic.

Page 16. A Test

The children should copy the questions in their Project Book and place the answers correctly in a column marked *Who or What*.
The correct answers are:

1. God
2. Creator
3. Creature
4. Creature
5. God
6. Men and angels
7. God
8. God
9. People
10. Beginning

Answers to the Tests: Book One

Page 20. A Bible Puzzle

Column A		Column B
1	is completed by	16
2	is completed by	12
3	is completed by	18
4	is completed by	11
5	is completed by	17
6	is completed by	14
7	is completed by	15
8	is completed by	13
9	is completed by	20
10	is completed by	19

Page 29. A Test

Column A		Column B
1	is completed by	13
2	is completed by	11
3	is completed by	8
4	is completed by	14
5	is completed by	9
6	is completed by	10
7	is completed by	12

Page 33. Three Kinds of Light

The words for the blank spaces:

1. sunlight
2. knowing
3. God
4. knowing
5. sunlight
6. God

Page 34. The Lights Which Show Us Beauty

The words for the blank spaces:
1. beautiful; beautiful
2. beauty; beauty; love
3. God's; God's; love

Page 36. Matching Test

The completed sentences:
1. God is Light.
2. The Light of God gives us the power to know God Himself.
3. Every best gift is from above, coming down from the Father of Lights.
4. God hath called you out of darkness into . . . light.
5. God, the Father of Lights, is the Source of all beauty.
6. God's Light in me gives me the power to see God's Beauty and to love Him.
7. When Saint James tells us that every best gift comes from the Father of Lights, he means that every best gift comes from God.
8. When The Bible tells us that God is Light, it does not mean light like the sunlight.

Page 37. Matching Test

The completed sentences:
1. God's Own Light and Beauty in me make me God's child.
2. The Light of Grace gives me the power to love and choose God.
3. The more I have of this Light of God, the more power I will have to know God Himself.
4. God's best gift to me is the Light of Grace.
5. God's Light of Grace in me gives me the power to see God's Beauty, and to love Him.
6. When I have the Light of Grace, God lets me share in His Own Light and Beauty.
7. When God's Own Light and Beauty are in me, God loves me tenderly.
8. God gave me the Light of Grace when I was baptized.
9. When God is my Loving Father, I belong with Him in His home in heaven.

Answers to the Tests: Book One

Page 41. My Soul and the Light of Grace
The words for the blank spaces:
1. soul   3. soul   5. baptized   7. Father   9. child
2. body   4. body   6. child   8. soul   10. created

Page 46. A Noble Prince or Princess
The words for the blank spaces:
   The sentence: Light; Beauty
   The motto: 1. King   3. kind
                2. brave   4. true

Page 50. Motto Test
1. true   2. kind   3. brave   4. brave   5. true

Page 63. A Bible Puzzle

Column A		Column B
1	is completed by	12
2	is completed by	11
3	is completed by	13
4	is completed by	14
5	is completed by	9
6	is completed by	8
7	is completed by	10

Page 69. True and False Test
Sentences that are true: 2, 6, 7, 8, 10
Sentences that are false: 1, 3, 4, 5, 9

Page 70. Matching Game

Column A		Column B
1	is completed by	9
2	is completed by	10
3	is completed by	6
4	is completed by	8
5	is completed by	7

The Spiritual Way: Manual

Page 72. True and False Test

True column: 1, 5, 7
False column: 2, 3, 4, 6

Page 74. How I Can Praise God

Be sure the children notice that the first letters of this exercise spell "Hallowed be Thy Name." The completed sentences are to begin with *I can praise God by*. For example, the first sentence will read: I can praise God by helping others to praise Him.

The words for the blank spaces:

H	Him	T	God
A	kind, true	H	in God's Light, Beauty
L	God	Y	missions
L	God		
O	God	N	prayers
W	God	A	God
E	God	M	God
D	me to do	E	God

B God
E be Thy Name

As an added exercise the teacher may have the children write other suggestions of ways in which they can praise God.

Page 77. Matching Game

Column A		Column B
1	is completed by	10
2	is completed by	6
3	is completed by	9
4	is completed by	7
5	is completed by	8

Answers to the Tests: Book One

Page 78. Three Problems

Problems are very valuable as applications of the doctrinal principle taught. The teacher will find it a practical and stimulating exercise for the children to solve additional problems appropriate to their own class experience.

Page 93. True and False Test

Have the children read the directions on page 93 very carefully, as they differ slightly from those given for the other true and false tests.
True sentences: 1, 4, 6
False sentences: 2, 3, 5, 7

Page 96. More Problems

The problems on pages 96 and 97 involve points of truth and honor in the schoolroom. Exercises of this kind should be used frequently to develop correct ideas of right and wrong in actual situations.
Have the children present problems to the class. Have a class discussion on the solution of these problems.

Page 108. Problems Answered by The Lord's Prayer

The words for the blank spaces:
1. Thy will be done on earth as it is in heaven.
2. Hallowed be Thy Name.
3. Lead us not into temptation.
4. Forgive us our trespasses as we forgive those who trespass against us.
5. Deliver us from evil.
6. Give us this day our daily bread.
7. Thy kingdom come.

BOOK TWO

Consult the directions given for the use of the tests on page 114 of the Manual.

Page 5. The First Man's Wonderful Gifts

After the children have completed the test, their books should be scored. This may be done by putting a list of correct answers on the board. Then have the children exchange books or correct their own.

The words for the blank spaces:

   1. image, likeness   4. mind, will
   2. mind   5. body
   3. will

Page 6. Question and Answer Test

Have the children read the directions very carefully. This exercise may be used as a class exercise, one child asking a question from Group I which another child answers from Group II. The next day the same exercise may be an individual exercise for the Project Book.

Group I		Group II
1	is answered by	7
2	is answered by	6
3	is answered by	5
4	is answered by	8

Page 7. Matching Test

After reading the directions carefully with the class, have the children divide a page of their Project Book in columns similar to those on page 8. Then have them copy in their Project Books the parts of sentences in Column A, completing the sentences from Column B.

Answers to the Tests: Book Two

The completed sentences:
1. The first man did not think and choose with his body.
2. The first man's mind and will were called powers of his soul.
3. With his mind the first man could think and know.
4. With his will the first man could love and choose.
5. God's very best gift to the first man let him share in God's Own Light and Beauty.
6. God's very best gift to the first man made him a child of God.
7. Because the first man was God's child, God was his Loving Father.
8. Because the first man was a child of God, he belonged with God in heaven.
9. God's image and likeness were in the first man because he had a mind, a will, and the Light of Grace in his soul.

After this exercise has been written, it may be used as an oral class exercise. The teacher may, for instance, call the name of one child in the class and give him a number from Column A. The child will read the text from Column A. Then either he or the teacher may ask another child to complete the sentence correctly.

Page 13. Matching Test

This test may be used in the same way as the preceding test.
The correct sentences:
1. A little boy or girl runs forward, with open arms, because his mind and his will are turned toward the person he loves.
2. When God's Own Light and Beauty are in my soul, my mind and will turn toward God with love, to think about Him and to know Him.
3. When anyone does not love God, his mind and his will are turned away from God.

The Spiritual Way: Manual

Page 15. The Mind, the Will, and the Light of Grace

The words for the blank spaces:
1. soul, body
2. gifts
3. mind, will, Light, Beauty

Page 19. A Problem Test

Column A: 4, 5
Column B: 1, 2, 3, 6

This test may be given first as an individual written exercise and afterwards as an oral class exercise with discussion.

Another set of problems similar to these might be given as a follow-up exercise to make sure that the principle that "the soul should rule the body" is grasped by the children. The pupils might also bring to the class for discussion other problems.

Page 29. Knowing God Better

In this completion test groups of words are given from which the child is to choose the right words to fill the blank spaces.

The words for the blank spaces:
1. the sky, the trees, the flowers
2. God
3. my father and mother, my teacher, the priest

Page 37. Ways of Serving God

The words for the blank spaces:
1. Commandments, Commandment
2. He, do
3. please

As an additional exercise the children may write lists of ways of serving God, such as:

Cheerful obedience at home and at school

Acts of kindness and of thoughtfulness toward others

Any act of self-control to please God

Answers to the Tests: Book Two

Page 38. True and False Test
True column: 2, 4
False column: 1, 3, 5
It would be a valuable exercise for the teacher to write a series of true and false statements pertaining to the home, the civic life of the child, and his school life. Problems of school discipline might be made the subject of such a test.

Page 39. Why God's Image and Likeness Are in You
The words for the blank spaces:
   1. know   2. love   3. serve

Page 43. True and False Test
True column: 1, 4   False column: 2, 3, 5
As with the test on page 38, the teacher may extend this test indefinitely.

Page 47. Acts Pleasing to God
The words for the blank spaces:
   1. Faith   2. Hope   3. Love   4. Contrition

Page 56. True and False Test
True column: 2, 3   False column: 1, 4, 5, 6

Page 63. True and False Test
True column: 1, 4, 6   False column: 2, 3, 5

Page 64. Heaven, Hell, and Purgatory
The words for the blank spaces:
1. Eye, ear, heart, God, love
2. fire, devil, angels
3. perfect, God, heaven, soul, body
4. evil
5. likeness, perfect, suffering
6. Light, Beauty, mind, will

124   The Spiritual Way: Manual

Page 69. A Test

This is an explanation test. Read the directions with the children very carefully. Group I consists of doctrinal points. The explanations of the doctrinal points are given in Group II.

The figures for the parenthesis:
(1) We belong to the Communion of Saints.
(3) I can offer to Our Heavenly Father my prayers and my good deeds to help the souls in purgatory.
(5) I can obtain blessings for my father and mother.
(4) I have a guardian angel.
(2) God wants us to love His angels and saints.

In order to impress the material in this test on the child's mind, the test should be used as both an oral and a written exercise.

Page 77. Problems

One of the best ways of impressing the Commandments on the child's mind is through the medium of problems. Exercises like this should be given throughout the study of the Commandments.

The Commandments to which the problems apply:
1. First Commandment
2. First Commandment
3. Fifth Commandment
   Second Commandment of the New Law
4. Second Commandment
5. Fourth Commandment

Page 83. A Prince Who Broke His Father's Law

The words to be supplied are:

1. rich
2. powerful
3. son
4. prince
5. kingdom
6. rule
7. priceless
8. die
9. study
10. love
11. happy
12. forever
13. obeying
14. choose
15. foolish
16. disobey
17. suffer
18. bad
19. work
20. share
21. family

Answers to the Tests: Book Two

Page 91. Matching Test

The directions given on page 120 of the Manual for the test on page 7 apply also to this test and the one on page 92.

The correct statements:

1. Adam, the father of all people, disobeyed God and lost his gift of sharing in God's Light and Beauty.
2. Because of Adam's disobedience, he no longer belonged in heaven with God.
3. Adam, with the gift of clear knowledge, failed to keep God's command, and lost the power to know without studying.
4. Adam chose to do what God told him not to do, and after that, he often felt like being bad, instead of being good.
5. After Adam disobeyed God, he often felt tired and suffered in many ways.
6. After Adam sinned, he could be sick, and he knew that sometime he must die.
7. Because of Adam's disobedience, God no longer visited with him.
8. Because Adam disobeyed God, he had to work very hard.
9. Because Adam disobeyed God's commands, the animals would no longer obey his commands.

Page 92.

The correct statements:

1. Because the father of all people sinned, we are said to be born in the state of original sin.
2. The father of all people lost the gift of sharing in God's Light and Beauty for himself and all other people.
3. After Adam sinned, he did not belong in heaven with God, neither did any of his family belong in heaven with God.
4. Because the father of all people disobeyed God, he lost the power to know and understand easily and quickly, and now all people must study if they wish to know and understand.

5. If Adam had not disobeyed God, there would not be such suffering and sorrow and unhappiness as there are in the world today.
6. Because the father of all people disobeyed God, he had to die, and now all people must die.
7. We must suffer because we are Adam's children.

Page 103. A Test

Use the directions given on page 124 of the Manual.
The figures for the parenthesis:

(6) "If any man violate the temple of God, him shall God destroy."

(5) God loves the virgin state.

(4) The King of Kings will not dwell within a soul that is disloyal and untrue through sins of impurity.

(3) My body is like a church.

(2) It is easy for the mind and will to be loyal and true guardians of God's temple when the Light of Grace is shining in the soul.

(1) The Light of Grace in the soul can be dimmed or put out entirely.

(10) If any evil person should try to tempt you to do something which would offend God, the Master of the temple, your mind would let you know the danger.

(9) I will keep my mind holy, my will holy, and my body holy, as long as I keep the Light of Grace shining brightly in my soul.

(8) I should pray to my Blessed Mother to help me to keep the Light of Grace so that my body will be a living temple for my God and King.

(7) If a bad companion tempts you to look at a picture or listen to a story which would cause your mind to become impure, you should have nothing to do with him.

Answers to the Tests: Book Two

Page 112. Yes and No Test

The correct answers:

1. Yes   3. No   5. Yes
2. No   4. No

Another valuable exercise might be made from this one by asking the children to give the reason for their Yes or No.

Page 116. Yes and No Test

The correct answers:

1. Yes   3. Yes   5. No   7. Yes
2. No   4. Yes   6. Yes

Page 117. Sin and Suffering

The correct choices:

1. by the way we use our wills to choose.
2. very great suffering follows.
3. he no longer shares in God's Light and Beauty.
4. his mind is darkened as to God and the things of God.
5. his will is turned away from God so that he does not choose God.
6. his mind will be darkened, and his will turned away from God forever.
7. he can never be in heaven with God.
8. he will be with the devils, and must suffer in hell forever.
9. his will is weakened.
10. when his will is weakened by many venial sins.
11. the one who tries hard not to commit venial sins.
12. some suffering follows every sin.
13. this state of suffering is called purgatory.

Page 123. Problems

Have the children read the problems carefully. Note that they are to tell which Commandment was kept, thus emphasizing the positive rather than the negative aspect.

The correct answers:
1. Seventh   3. Second   5. Sixth   7. Fifth
2. Third   4. Tenth   6. First   8. Eighth

It would be well to give the child many problems which bring home to him the meaning of the Commandments, particularly the Fourth Commandment.

BOOK THREE

Page 2. Yes and No Test

The correct answers:
1. Yes   3. No   5. No
2. Yes   4. Yes

Page 4. A Mystery Puzzle

The correct answers:
1. we call it a mystery.
2. from a little seed.
3. we could never know.
4. that we cannot fully understand.
5. we show that we have faith.
6. shall be saved.
7. impossible to please God.
8. we should believe mysteries made known by God.

Page 8. Question and Answer Test

Have the child read the directions carefully, noting that the answers are in Group I and the questions in Group II.

The figures for the parenthesis:

(10) No   (8) Catechism
(9) God   (4) Intellect
(5) Angels   (7) St. Thomas
(3) Doctor of the Church   (1) A spirit
(6) St. John 4:24   (2) The soul

This test may also be used to advantage as an oral exercise.

Answers to the Tests: Book Three

Page 12. A Dialogue Lesson

The answers:
1. I am a human being.
2. The mystery of the Blessed Trinity is the greatest of all mysteries.
3. There is but one God.
4. The three Divine Persons are equal.
5. The three Divine Persons in God are separate.

Page 19. A Bible Test

The teacher will note that the child is given a double exercise: (1) to match the parts of the text correctly; (2) to place the texts in columns under the correct heading.

When more than one Person of the Blessed Trinity is mentioned, the text may be placed in both columns or in the one to which it more expressly refers. The correctly matched texts grouped in the second way are given below. Have the child write them in full.

The Father	The Son	The Holy Ghost
1. 2 St. Peter 1 : 17	3. Acts 8 : 37	2. St. Luke 12 : 12
	4. St. John 5 : 23	
	5. St. Matthew 16 : 16	

This test may be extended by choosing other Bible texts. Here are a few additional ones:

St. Matthew 11 : 27   1 St. John 4 : 15   St. Matthew 10 : 32
1 Corinthians 6 : 19   Acts 2 : 4

Page 32. Before and After Test

Column A : 2, 3, 5, 7, 10, 11, 13
Column B : 1, 4, 6, 8, 9, 12, 14
This test should also be given as an oral lesson.

The Spiritual Way: Manual

Page 37. A Matching Test

1 is completed by 8.   4 is completed by 11.
2 is completed by 9.   5 is completed by 7.
3 is completed by 10.   6 is completed by 12.

Page 40. Another Matching Test

1 is completed by 12.   4 is completed by 8.
2 is completed by 9.   5 is completed by 11.
3 is completed by 10.   6 is completed by 7.

Page 44. A Matching Test

1 is completed by 7.   4 is completed by 9.
2 is completed by 11.   5 is completed by 10.
3 is completed by 12.   6 is completed by 8.

Page 46. The Second Part of the Apostles' Creed

The correctly matched pictures and texts:
1 belongs with picture J.
2 belongs with picture G.
3 belongs with picture L.
4 belongs with picture N.
5 belongs with picture P.
6 belongs with picture Q.

Page 50. Jesus Chose to Suffer — Why?

This test differs from the other explanation tests in that the explanations are all Bible texts.

Group I		Group II
1	is explained by	5
2	is explained by	3
3	is explained by	1
4	is explained by	2
5	is explained by	4
6	is explained by	6

Answers to the Tests: Book Three

7	is explained by	8
8	is explained by	10
9	is explained by	9
10	is explained by	7

Page 52. A Calendar Test

As the days mentioned are all movable feasts, the answers for the third column are not given here.

The answers for the second column:
1. Good Friday
2. Easter Sunday
3. Ascension Thursday

Practically all the feasts in the Church calendar might be made the subject of a test such as this.

Page 53. A Bible Hunt

The answers in the second column:

2. St. John 4 : 46–54. Jesus heals at a distance the ruler's son who is ill at Capharnaum.

3. St. Matthew 8 : 23–27. Jesus commands the winds and the seas and they become calm.

4. St. John 5 : 1–17. At the pool of Bethsaida Jesus heals the man who has been sick for thirty-eight years and who has had no one to put him into the pond.

5. St. Matthew 8 : 5–17. Jesus heals the centurion's servant. Jesus heals Peter's wife's mother. Jesus heals many who are sick.

6. St. Luke 7 : 11–18. Jesus restores to life the son of the widow of Naim.

7. St. John 9 : 1–42. Jesus spreads clay upon the eyes of the man born blind and sends him to wash in the pool of Siloe, after which his sight is restored.

8. St. Matthew 26 : 36–47. Jesus goes to the garden of Gethsemani and suffers a cruel agony.

9. St. John 18 : 1-12. Judas betrays Jesus. The soldiers take Jesus, bind Him, and lead Him away.
10. St. Luke 23 : 32-44. Jesus is crucified between two thieves.
11. St. Mark 16 : 1-11. Mary Magdalen and the other holy women go to Jesus' tomb and find that He is risen. He appears to Mary Magdalen.
12. St. Luke 24 : 50-53. Jesus goes with His Apostles to Bethania, blesses them, and ascends into heaven.
13. St. Matthew 6 : 1-15. Jesus teaches His Apostles how to pray. He teaches them the Our Father.

What the text tells may be enlarged upon. Merely the salient points are given here.

Page 69. A Find-Out-Why Test

The five sentences may be completed by *she is the Mother of God*.

Page 69. Which One Is She?

Mary: 1, 4, 5, 7 *Any other woman:* 2, 3, 6

Page 72. A Story Puzzle

The numbers of the questions with the numbers in the story which answer them:

1 is answered by 7.   8 is answered by 2.
2 is answered by 11.   9 is answered by 12.
3 is answered by 10.   10 is answered by 1.
4 is answered by 6.   11 is answered by 4.
5 is answered by 13.   12 is answered by 3.
6 is answered by 8.   13 is answered by 5.
7 is answered by 14.   14 is answered by 9.

Page 75. Hail, Full of Grace

Group II		Group I
1	is completed by	2
2	is completed by	1
3	is completed by	5

Answers to the Tests: Book Three

4	is completed by	3
5	is completed by	6
6	is completed by	4

Page 80. Another Story Puzzle

The numbers of the questions with the numbers in the story which answer them:

1 is answered by 2.	5 is answered by 4.
2 is answered by 6.	6 is answered by 7.
3 is answered by 8.	7 is answered by 1.
4 is answered by 5.	8 is answered by 3.

Page 89. Honoring the Blessed Virgin Mary

Column A		Column B
1	is completed by	7
2	is completed by	1
3	is completed by	6
4	is completed by	3
5	is completed by	4
6	is completed by	2
7	is completed by	8
8	is completed by	5

Page 98. A Test

What column		Answer column
1	is answered by	4
2	is answered by	5
3	is answered by	1
4	is answered by	6
5	is answered by	8
6	is answered by	7
7	is answered by	9
8	is answered by	10
9	is answered by	3
10	is answered by	2

Page 101. A Test

What column		Answer column
1	is answered by	2
2	is answered by	4
3	is answered by	1
4	is answered by	5
5	is answered by	3

Page 107. A Test

Five headings are given concerning the Passover. The child is asked to place under each heading the two parts of sentences which will make correct complete sentences with this heading.

Headings		Parts of sentences
B	is completed by	1 and 5
C	is completed by	4 and 9
D	is completed by	3 and 8
E	is completed by	6 and 10

Page 111. A Test

The word which answers each of the five questions is *obedient*.

Page 112. A Bible Hunt

The teacher will note that the five texts given below all refer to Abraham's obedience and faith.

St. John 8 : 39. Jesus saith to them: If you be the children of Abraham, do the works of Abraham.

St. James 2 : 21, 23. Was not Abraham our father justified by works, offering up Isaac his son upon the altar? And the scripture was fulfilled, saying: Abraham believed God, and it was reputed to him to justice, and he was called the friend of God.

Hebrews 11 : 8. By faith he that is called Abraham, obeyed to go out into a place which he was to receive for an inheritance; and he went out, not knowing whither he went.

Answers to the Tests: Book Three

Galatians 3 : 9. Therefore they that are of faith, shall be blessed with faithful Abraham.

Hebrews 11 : 17. By faith Abraham, when he was tried, offered Isaac: and he that had received the promises, offered up his only begotten son.

Page 112. A Test

Have the children read the directions very carefully. The teacher will notice that the test tells about kings, prophets, and holy men of the Old Law who offered sacrifices to God. The children are asked to write the Bible text under the name of the man who offered the sacrifice. They are not asked to classify as to kings, prophets, and holy men, but this might be used as an additional exercise. The correct matching:

Cain.   1 is completed by 8.
Abel.   2 is completed by 6.
Noë.   3 is completed by 2.
Samuel.   4 is completed by 1.
David.   5 is completed by 3.
Melchisedech.   6 is completed by 4.
Abraham.   7 is completed by 5.
Solomon.   8 is completed by 7.

The one sacrifice that was not acceptable was that of Cain.

In the beginning of his life Solomon was pleasing to God, but later on he was unfaithful.

David, Solomon, and Melchisedech were kings.

Page 117. A Test

This is a suggestive type of test which might be used in working out any Bible story.

The correct answers:
1. Peter, John
2. Jesus
3. The goodman of the house

4. A man carrying a pitcher
5. Peter, John.

Page 120. A Test

This test is designed to show the union between the Old and the New Law, for the sacrifice of the paschal lamb in the Old Law prefigured the Sacrifice of Jesus, the true Lamb, in the New Law. The prophecy of Isaias pictures Jesus as a lamb.

In the first column of the test a quality of the lamb is given. In the second column there is a prophecy of Isaias foretelling this lamb-like quality in Jesus. In the third column texts from the New Testament are given which show that Jesus has this quality.

Each correct Bible text counts 5.

1. *Meekness*

1 St. Peter 2 : 23.   Who, when he was reviled, did not revile : when he suffered, he threatened not : but delivered himself to him that judged him unjustly.

St. Luke 23 : 33, 34.   And when they were come to the place which is called Calvary, they crucified him there ; and the robbers, one on the right hand, and the other on the left.

And Jesus said : Father, forgive them, for they know not what they do.   But they, dividing his garments, cast lots.

St. Luke 22 : 47, 48.   As he was yet speaking, behold a multitude ; and he that was called Judas, one of the twelve, went before them, and drew near to Jesus, for to kiss him.

And Jesus said to him : Judas, dost thou betray the Son of man with a kiss ?

St. John 13 : 13–15.   You call me Master, and Lord ; and you say well, for so I am.

If then I being your Lord and Master, have washed your feet ; you also ought to wash one another's feet.

For I have given you an example, that as I have done to you, so you do also.

Answers to the Tests: Book Three

2. *Silence*

St. Matthew 27 : 12-14. And when he was accused by the chief priests and ancients, he answered nothing.

Then Pilate saith to him: Dost not thou hear how great testimonies they allege against thee?

And he answered him to never a word; so that the governor wondered exceedingly.

St. Mark 15 : 3-5. And the chief priests accused him in many things.

And Pilate again asked him, saying: Answerest thou nothing? behold in how many things they accuse thee.

But Jesus still answered nothing; so that Pilate wondered.

St. John 19 : 7-9. The Jews answered him: We have a law; and according to the law he ought to die, because he made himself the Son of God.

When Pilate therefore had heard this saying, he feared the more.

And he entered into the hall again, and he said to Jesus: Whence art thou? But Jesus gave him no answer.

St. Luke 23 : 9-11. And he questioned him in many words. But he answered him nothing.

And the chief priests and the scribes stood by, earnestly accusing him.

And Herod with his army set him at nought, and mocked him, putting on him a white garment, and sent him back to Pilate.

3. *Innocence*

St. Luke 23 : 22. And he said to them the third time: Why, what evil hath this man done? I find no cause of death in him. I will chastise him therefore, and let him go.

St. Luke 23 : 39-41. And one of those robbers who were hanged, blasphemed him, saying: If thou be Christ, save thyself and us.

But the other answering, rebuked him, saying: Neither dost thou fear God, seeing thou art under the same condemnation?

And we indeed justly, for we receive the due reward of our deeds; but this man hath done no evil.

St. John 15 : 25. But that the word may be fulfilled which is written in their law: They hated me without cause.

St. John 19 : 4. Pilate therefore went forth again, and saith to them: Behold, I bring him forth unto you, that you may know I find no cause in him.

4. *Readiness for sacrifice*

St. John 18 : 36, 37. Jesus answered: My kingdom is not of this world. If my kingdom were of this world, my servants would certainly strive that I should not be delivered to the Jews: but now my kingdom is not from hence.

Pilate therefore said to him: Art thou a king then? Jesus answered: Thou sayest that I am a king. For this was I born, and for this came I into the world; that I should give testimony to the truth. Every one that is of the truth, heareth my voice.

St. John 18 : 11. Jesus therefore said to Peter: Put up thy sword into the scabbard. The chalice which my Father hath given me, shall I not drink it?

St. Matthew 26 : 53, 54. Thinkest thou that I cannot ask my Father, and he will give me presently more than twelve legions of angels?

How then shall the scriptures be fulfilled, that so it must be done?

St. John 19 : 11. Jesus answered: Thou shouldst not have any power against me, unless it were given thee from above. Therefore, he that hath delivered me to thee, hath the greater sin.

5. *Suffering*

St. Matthew 26 : 67, 68. Then did they spit in his face, and buffeted him: and others struck his face with the palms of their hands,

Answers to the Tests: Book Three

Saying: Prophesy unto us, O Christ, who is he that struck thee?

St. Luke 22 : 63-65. And the men that held him, mocked him, and struck him.

And they blindfolded him, and smote his face. And they asked him, saying: Prophesy, who is it that struck thee?

And blaspheming, many other things they said against him.

St. John 19 : 1-3. Then therefore, Pilate took Jesus, and scourged him.

And the soldiers platting a crown of thorns, put it upon his head; and they put on him a purple garment.

And they came to him, and said: Hail, king of the Jews; and they gave him blows.

St. Mark 15 : 16-20. And the soldiers led him away into the court of the palace, and they called together the whole band:

And they clothed him with purple, and platting a crown of thorns, they put it upon him.

And they began to salute him: Hail, king of the Jews.

And they struck his head with a reed: and they did spit on him. And bowing their knees, they adored him.

And after they had mocked him, they took off the purple from him, and put his own garments on him, and they led him out to crucify him.

Page 129. A Test

It is very essential for the Catholic to understand that the priesthood of Jesus did not cease with His death on the Cross, where He was both Priest and Victim.

First column		Second column
1	is completed by	8
2	is completed by	9
3	is completed by	5
4	is completed by	1
5	is completed by	2

6	is completed by	4
7	is completed by	3
8	is completed by	7
9	is completed by	10
10	is completed by	6

Page 130. A Test

Column A: 4, 8, 13   Column D: 6, 10, 14
Column B: 2, 11, 18   Column E: 1, 7, 9
Column C: 3, 15, 17   Column F: 5, 12, 16

This is an appreciation lesson, in test form, on the Holy Sacrifice of the Mass. Appreciation lessons are used by many good teachers in music, art, and other subjects. It is most fitting that this form of lesson should be given to help the child see the value and the beauty of this central act of Catholic worship.

Page 134. The Most Solemn Part of the Sacrifice

The correct words for the blank spaces:

1. Consecration
2. Jesus
3. middle
4. prepare
5. Jesus, bread, wine
6. Consecration
7. ourselves, others
8. departed
9. Commemoration, me
10. thanks, brake, Apostles

Page 138. The Complete Action in the Offering of the Holy Sacrifice of the Mass

Diagrams are very helpful in enabling children to clarify their own ideas because a diagram, if correctly made, makes clear the important and subordinate parts of the subject diagramed.

It is very necessary that the children should have clearly in mind what is the essential part of the Sacrifice of the Mass and what is not essential to the Sacrifice. They should also understand how the preparation and thanksgiving are related to the essential part of the Mass.

In the first diagram on page 138 a triangle is used because it illustrates so well the proper relationship of the parts of the Mass.

The words "Do This in Commemoration of Me" are written on the base of this isosceles triangle to show that the continuous offering of the Holy Sacrifice of the Mass rests on this command given by Our Lord at the Last Supper.

The word "Preparation" is written on one side of the triangle and "Thanksgiving" on the other side. The words "Consecration and Communion" are written at the apex of the triangle. The Preparation leads toward this apex; the Thanksgiving, away from it.

The first diagram is the skeleton showing the parts of the Mass. The second shows how we should enter into the different parts of the Mass.

We cannot enter into anything without activity. And to enter into or take part in the Holy Sacrifice of the Mass we must *Be Active*.

The second diagram is not designed to tell what prayers to say, but to indicate the spirit with which these prayers should be said. For in the Missal the prayers of the preparation in the main express sentiments of contrition, faith, and oblation. Therefore during preparation, one's activity should be expressed through contrition, faith, and oblation.

The theological virtues of faith, hope, and love relate directly to God, and so it is fitting that the prayers said at the most solemn part of the Mass should express sentiments of faith, hope, and love.

The prayers in the Missal for the latter part of the Mass are prayers filled with sentiments of love and gratitude, and the activity during this part of the Mass should be expressed in this form.

Page 139. A Missal Hunt

After the child has been taught the structure of the Mass and the spirit animating the prayers said during the different parts, he should be taught to say the prayers given in the Missal, always remembering to keep the prayers animated by the spirit of the acts.

As the Missal gives in translation the actual prayers said by the priest in the Mass of each day, there is no better way of assisting at Mass than by intelligently and actively participating in the Sacrifice with the priest.

Preparation: 1, 5, 6, 10, 13, 17, 20
Consecration and Communion: 2, 3, 7, 9, 11, 12, 15, 16, 18, 19
Thanksgiving: 4, 8, 14

Page 146. Another Missal Hunt

The teacher will note that the four ends of Sacrifice are given here. The child is asked to place twelve prayers from the Missal under the appropriate headings. This test is designed to give the child a further understanding of the prayers of the Missal and to enable him to appreciate that these prayers have been written with the four ends of the Sacrifice in view, so that those who use these prayers intelligently will be helped to enter actively into the spirit of the Mass.

Adoration and praise: 1, 7, 9
Thanksgiving: 2, 5, 11
Atonement or satisfaction for sin: 4, 6, 10
Petition for graces and blessings: 3, 8, 12

Page 151. A Test

Praise
    St. Luke 19 : 37, 38   Hebrews 13 : 15   St. Luke 2 : 13, 14
    St. Luke 24 : 52, 53   Apocalypse 19 : 5
Thanksgiving
    1 Corinthians 11 : 24   (This might also be under *Atonement.*)
    Apocalypse 11 : 17
    St. Luke 17 : 12–19
    1 Thessalonians 5 : 18
    Ephesians 5 : 19, 20 (5 : 19 might also be under *Praise.*)

Answers to the Tests: Book Three 143

Atonement or Propitiation
1 Peter 3 : 18   Romans 3 : 25   Romans 5 : 9
Romans 5 : 19   1 St. John 2 : 2
Prayer of Petition
St. Luke 11 : 2-4   St. Matthew 26 : 39   St. Luke 23 : 34
St. Luke 11 : 9, 10   Acts 7 : 58, 59

1. *Praise*

St. Luke 19 : 37, 38. And when he was now coming near the descent of mount Olivet, the whole multitude of his disciples began with joy to praise God with a loud voice, for all the mighty works they had seen,

Saying: Blessed be the king who cometh in the name of the Lord, peace in heaven, and glory on high!

St. Luke 24 : 52, 53. And they adoring went back into Jerusalem with great joy.

And they were always in the temple, praising and blessing God. Amen.

Hebrews 13 : 15. By him therefore let us offer the sacrifice of praise always to God, that is to say, the fruit of lips confessing to his name.

Apocalypse 19 : 5. And a voice came out from the throne, saying: Give praise to our God, all ye his servants; and you that fear him, little and great.

St. Luke 2 : 13, 14. And suddenly there was with the angel a multitude of the heavenly army, praising God, and saying:

Glory to God in the highest; and on earth peace to men of good will.

2. *Thanksgiving*

1 Corinthians 11 : 24. And giving thanks, broke, and said: Take ye, and eat: this is my body, which shall be delivered for you: this do for the commemoration of me.

Apocalypse 11 : 17. We give thee thanks, O Lord God Almighty, who art, and who wast, and who art to come: because thou hast taken to thee thy great power, and thou hast reigned.

St. Luke 17 : 12–19. And as he entered into a certain town, there met him ten men that were lepers, who stood afar off;

And lifted up their voice, saying: Jesus, master, have mercy on us.

Whom when he saw, he said: Go, shew yourselves to the priests. And it came to pass, as they went, they were made clean.

And one of them, when he saw that he was made clean, went back, with a loud voice glorifying God.

And he fell on his face before his feet, giving thanks: and this was a Samaritan.

And Jesus answering, said, Were not ten made clean? and where are the nine?

There is no one found to return and give glory to God, but this stranger.

And he said to him: Arise, go thy way; for thy faith hath made thee whole.

1 Thessalonians 5 : 18. In all things give thanks; for this is the will of God in Christ Jesus concerning you all.

Ephesians 5 : 19, 20. Speaking to yourselves in psalms, and hymns, and spiritual canticles, singing and making melody in your hearts to the Lord;

Giving thanks always for all things, in the name of our Lord Jesus Christ, to God and the Father.

3. *Atonement or Propitiation*

1 St. Peter 3 : 18. Because Christ also died once for our sins, the just for the unjust: that he might offer us to God, being put to death indeed in the flesh, but enlivened in the spirit.

Romans 5 : 19. For as by the disobedience of one man, many

were made sinners; so also by the obedience of one, many shall be made just.

Romans 3 : 25. Whom God hath proposed to be a propitiation, through faith in his blood, to the shewing of his justice, for the remission of former sins.

1 St. John 2 : 2. And he is the propitiation for our sins: and not for ours only, but also for those of the whole world.

Romans 5 : 9. Christ died for us; much more therefore, being now justified by his blood, shall we be saved from wrath through him.

4. *Prayer of Petition*

St. Luke 11 : 2-4. And he said to them: When you pray, say: Father, hallowed be thy name. Thy kingdom come.

Give us this day our daily bread.

And forgive us our sins, for we also forgive every one that is indebted to us. And lead us not into temptation.

St. Luke 11 : 9, 10. And I say to you, Ask, and it shall be given you: seek, and you shall find: knock, and it shall be opened to you.

For every one that asketh, receiveth; and he that seeketh, findeth; and to him that knocketh, it shall be opened.

St. Matthew 26 : 39. And going a little further, he fell upon his face, praying, and saying: My Father, if it be possible, let this chalice pass from me. Nevertheless not as I will, but as thou wilt.

Acts 7 : 58, 59. And they stoned Stephen, invoking, and saying: Lord Jesus, receive my spirit.

And falling on his knees, he cried with a loud voice, saying: Lord, lay not this sin to their charge. And when he had said this, he fell alseep in the Lord. And Saul was consenting to his death.

St. Luke 23 : 34. And Jesus said: Father, forgive them, for they know not what they do. But they, dividing his garments, cast lots.

BOOK FOUR

Page 6. True and False Test

The true sentences: 3, 5, 7, 8, 10

The false sentences: 1, 2, 4, 6, 9

Page 11. A Test

In this test the time element is introduced because a child should be trained to think both accurately and quickly.

It is advisable to acquaint the children with this kind of work before giving it to them as a written test. For this reason it would be best to use this test as an oral exercise first. Give half the test for thirty minutes, then the other half, and finally the whole test.

This type of test is usually interesting to children, and the teacher will find it a useful way to test the children's knowledge of any Bible texts.

Punctuation has not been included in the test. The proper marks may be inserted by the children, but the punctuation should not be considered as right or wrong in scoring the test.

The completed sentences:

1. Behold I am with you all days.
2. And I say to thee: That thou art Peter; and upon this rock I will build my church.
3. And thou, being once converted, confirm thy brethren.
4. All power is given to me in heaven and in earth.
5. The gates of hell shall not prevail against it.
6. Simon, Simon, behold satan hath desired to have you, that he may sift you as wheat.
7. Going therefore, teach ye all nations; baptizing them in the name of the Father, and of the Son, and of the Holy Ghost.
8. And I will give to thee the keys of the kingdom of heaven.
9. As the Father hath sent me, I also send you.
10. And whatsoever thou shalt bind upon earth, it shall be bound also in heaven.

11. But I have prayed for thee, that thy faith fail not.
12. And whatsoever thou shalt loose on earth, it shall be loosed also in heaven.

Page 15. A Bible Hunt

St. John 10 : 11. Jesus tells us that He is the Good Shepherd and that He gives His Life for His sheep.

St. Luke 15 : 4–6. If the Good Shepherd has one hundred sheep and loses one of them, He will leave the ninety-nine to search for the one that is lost. Great rejoicing follows the finding of the lost sheep.

St. John 10 : 12, 13. The hireling protects himself and leaves the sheep to perish when there is danger. The Good Shepherd does not do this.

1 St. Peter 2 : 25. Before the coming of Jesus the human race were as sheep going astray, but now many have followed the true Shepherd.

St. John 10 : 14, 15. Jesus as Good Shepherd tells us that He knows His sheep and His sheep know Him and that He lays down His Life for His sheep.

St. John 21 : 15. Jesus says to Peter: "Feed my lambs."

St. John 10 : 16. Jesus tells us that there are many sheep which belong to Him but are not in His fold. He says these sheep will hear His voice and there will be one fold and one Shepherd.

St. John 10 : 2, 3. Jesus says that the shepherd enters into the sheepfold by the door. "The sheep hear his voice: and he calleth his own sheep by name, and leadeth them out."

Page 15. A Matching Test

First column		Second column
1	is completed by	8
2	is completed by	1
3	is completed by	7
4	is completed by	2

5	is completed by	4
6	is completed by	5
7	is completed by	3
8	is completed by	6

Other texts may be added to the tests.

Page 18. Which Mark Is It?

The words for the blank spaces:
    1. One   4. Apostolic   7. Holy
    2. Holy   5. One, Catholic
    3. Catholic   6. Apostolic

Page 18. Which Marks of Jesus' Church Are Missing?
    1. Apostolic   3. Holy   5. Catholic
    2. Apostolic or Holy   4. One

Page 20. A Test

1. The Feast of All Saints comes November 1. We celebrate the glory of all the Saints.

2. The feast of New Year's Day comes January 1. We celebrate Our Lord's receiving the name *Jesus*.

3. The feast of Christmas comes December 25. We celebrate the Nativity of Our Lord.

4. The feast of the Ascension comes —— this year. We celebrate Jesus' going up into heaven by His Own power.

5. The feast of the Assumption comes on August 15. We celebrate the taking up of the Blessed Virgin Mary, both body and soul, into heaven.

6. The feast of the Immaculate Conception comes on December 8. We celebrate a feast honoring the Blessed Virgin Mary because she was never in the state of original sin.

Page 23. Some Problems to Solve

1. Eva broke the third Commandment of Holy Church for several months.

Answers to the Tests: Book Four

2. Because John did not receive the Holy Eucharist during Easter time, he breaks the fourth Commandment of Holy Church.
3. To obey the Church and her mother, Catherine must get up and go to an early Mass.
4. The first Commandment of Holy Church is to hear Mass on Sundays and holy days of obligation.
5. Miss Wilson obeyed the sixth Commandment of Holy Church.
6. You should refuse the chicken sandwiches.
7. Mr. Scott and his family do not observe the fifth Commandment of Holy Church.

Page 26. A Test

1	is completed by	6	6	is completed by	3
2	is completed by	4	7	is completed by	5
3	is completed by	1	8	is completed by	10
4	is completed by	9	9	is completed by	2
5	is completed by	7	10	is completed by	8

Page 29. A Test

1	is completed by	4	3	is completed by	2
2	is completed by	1	4	is completed by	3

Page 30. A Test

1	is completed by	4	4	is completed by	2
2	is completed by	1	5	is completed by	3
3	is completed by	5			

Page 34. A Test

1	is called	9	6	is called	3
2	is called	4	7	is called	8
3	is called	10	8	is called	1
4	is called	5	9	is called	7
5	is called	2	10	is called	6

Page 47. A Test
The correct answers:
1. Seven
2. Jesus' Church
3. By a special sign
4. The Sacraments
5. Jesus' priests
6. Jesus
7. Divine Life.
8. God's Own Light and Beauty
9. The water of life
10. A fountain

Page 51. A Test
The true sentences: 2, 4, 6, 7, 8, 9, 10

Page 57. A Test
It will be interesting for the children to make a comparison as to their rights as citizens of earth and citizens of heaven.

The teacher will note that in the first part of the exercise the children are asked to think of points about Baptism which are similar to the points given about the flag. In the second part, or as a second exercise, they are asked to compare their points with the points given in the text. Then they are to write the points of comparison as given in the text in two columns in their Project Book.

Page 61. A Test
The words for the blank spaces:
1. Bishops and priests
2. Any person
3. Sponsor
4. Parent
5. Private Baptism
6. Godfather or godmother
7. Once
8. Divine Life
9. Being born again
10. Jesus

Page 64. A Test
The children are expected to use the form given on page 151 in carrying out the directions for the test.

Answers to the Tests: Book Four

What the priest does	What the priest says	What the one to be baptized, or his sponsor, says and does
1. —	John, what dost thou ask of the Church of God?	Faith
2. —	What doth faith bring thee to?	Life everlasting
3. —	If, therefore, thou wilt enter into life, keep the Commandments. Thou shalt love the Lord thy God with all thy heart, and with all thy soul and with all thy mind, and thy neighbor as thyself.	—
4. He breathes upon the face of the one being baptized.	Depart from him, thou unclean spirit, and give place to the Holy Ghost, the Paraclete.	—

Page 70. A Test

1	is answered by	9	7	is answered by	10
2	is answered by	5	8	is answered by	11
3	is answered by	1	9	is answered by	12
4	is answered by	8	10	is answered by	7
5	is answered by	6	11	is answered by	2
6	is answered by	3	12	is answered by	4

Page 82. True and False Test

The false sentences: 4, 8, 10, 13, 15

Page 94. True and False Test

The true statements: 2, 8, 9, 10

The false statements: 1, 3, 4, 5, 6, 7

Page 100. A Test

The correct choices:
1. I will make an Act of Contrition and tell the sin in my next Confession.
2. Jesus would know that I concealed it.
3. My Confessions will increase my sins.
4. My sins will not be forgiven.
5. No priest ever tells what he hears in Confession.
6. He loved us and wanted us to return His Love.

Page 107. A Test

The numbers for the parenthesis:
(6) Temporal punishment.
(1) A penance.
(4) Suffering and sacrifice lovingly accepted.
(3) The satisfaction for sin required by the law of justice.
(5) To meet the requirements of the law of justice.
(2) Everlasting punishment.

Page 110. A Test

1	is completed by	3	4	is completed by	4
2	is completed by	5	5	is completed by	2
3	is completed by	1			

Page 112. A Test

The correct choices:
1. to bind and loose.
2. the Church accepted the sufferings of the martyrs in place of canonical penances.
3. the temporal punishment due to sin.
4. he believed that his sufferings could help the other members of the Mystical Body of Christ.
5. everyone who has the Light of Grace in his soul can add to the spiritual treasury of the Church.

Answers to the Tests: Book Four

Page 116. True and False Test

True sentences: 2, 4, 6, 7, 8   False sentences: 1, 3, 5

Page 122. A Test

The Eucharistic Lamb offered in sacrifice is the only adequate worship of God.

The Eucharistic Lamb offered in sacrifice is the only adequate atonement to God.

The Eucharistic Lamb offered in sacrifice is the only adequate thanksgiving to God.

The Eucharistic Lamb offered in sacrifice obtains greatest blessings from God.

The Eucharistic Lamb, the daily Food for all people, increases Divine Life when received with love.

The Eucharistic Lamb, the daily Food for all people, increases holiness when received with love.

The Eucharistic Lamb, the daily Food for all people, increases spiritual power when received with love.

The Eucharistic Lamb, the daily Food for all people, brings graces and blessings when received with love.

Page 125. A Miracle Story Test

The numbers of the questions with the numbers in the story which answer them:

1 is answered by 10.	11 is answered by 19.
2 is answered by 13.	12 is answered by 2.
3 is answered by 11.	13 is answered by 9.
4 is answered by 16.	14 is answered by 7.
5 is answered by 20.	15 is answered by 4.
6 is answered by 3.	16 is answered by 12.
7 is answered by 15.	17 is answered by 8.
8 is answered by 18.	18 is answered by 6.
9 is answered by 1.	19 is answered by 14.
10 is answered by 5.	20 is answered by 17.

The Spiritual Way: Manual

Page 129. A Test

1	is answered by	4		5	is answered by	7
2	is answered by	5		6	is answered by	6
3	is answered by	2		7	is answered by	3
4	is answered by	1				

Page 130. A Test

The Bible texts:

St. John 6 : 52. If any man eat of this bread, he shall live for ever; and the bread that I will give, is my flesh, for the life of the world.

1 Corinthians 10 : 17. For we, being many, are one bread, one body, all that partake of one bread.

St. Luke 11 : 3. Give us this day our daily bread.

St. John 6 : 56, 59. For my flesh is meat indeed : and my blood is drink indeed.

This is the bread that came down from heaven. Not as your fathers did eat manna, and are dead. He that eateth this bread, shall live forever.

1 Corinthians 11 : 24, 25. And giving thanks, broke, and said : Take ye, and eat : this is my body, which shall be delivered for you : this do for the commemoration of me.

In like manner also the chalice, after he had supped, saying : This chalice is the new testament in my blood : this do ye, as often as you shall drink, for the commemoration of me.

St. Matthew 26 : 26, 27, 28. And whilst they were at supper, Jesus took bread, and blessed, and broke : and gave to his disciples, and said : Take ye, and eat. This is my body.

And taking the chalice, he gave thanks, and gave to them, saying : Drink ye all of this.

For this is my blood of the new testament, which shall be shed for many unto remission of sins.

Answers to the Tests: Book Four

St. John 6 : 32, 33. Then Jesus said to them: Amen, amen I say to you; Moses gave you not bread from heaven, but my Father giveth you the true bread from heaven.

For the bread of God is that which cometh down from heaven, and giveth life to the world.

1 Corinthians 10 : 16. The chalice of benediction, which we bless, is it not the communion of the blood of Christ? And the bread, which we break, is it not the partaking of the body of the Lord?

St. John 6 : 48. I am the bread of life.

St. Luke 22 : 17, 18, 19, 20. And having taken the chalice, he gave thanks, and said: Take, and divide it among you:

For I say to you, that I will not drink of the fruit of the vine, till the kingdom of God come.

And taking bread, he gave thanks, and brake; and gave to them, saying: This is my body, which is given for you. Do this for a commemoration of me.

In like manner the chalice also, after he had supped, saying: This is the chalice, the new testament in my blood, which shall be shed for you.

St. John 6 : 54, 55. Then Jesus said to them: Amen, amen I say unto you: Except you eat the flesh of the Son of man, and drink his blood, you shall not have life in you.

He that eateth my flesh, and drinketh my blood, hath everlasting life: and I will raise him up in the last day.

1 Corinthians 11 : 28, 29. But let a man prove himself: and so let him eat of that bread, and drink of the chalice.

For he that eateth and drinketh unworthily, eateth and drinketh judgment to himself, not discerning the body of the Lord.

St. John 6 : 35. And Jesus said to them: I am the bread of life: he that cometh to me shall not hunger: and he that believeth in me shall never thirst.

St. Mark 14 : 22, 23, 24. And whilst they were eating, Jesus took bread; and blessing, broke, and gave to them, and said: Take ye. This is my body.

And having taken the chalice, giving thanks, he gave it to them. And they all drank of it.

And he said to them: This is my blood of the new testament, which shall be shed for many.

1 Corinthians 11 : 26, 27. For as often as you shall eat this bread, and drink the chalice, you shall shew the death of the Lord, until he come.

Therefore whosoever shall eat this bread, or drink the chalice of the Lord unworthily, shall be guilty of the body and of the blood of the Lord.

Page 134. True and False Test

The true sentences: 1, 2, 6
The false sentences: 3, 4, 5, 7

Page 148. The Sacrament of Matrimony

The words for the blank spaces:
1. holy, God
2. Sacrament, grace
3. Matrimony, death
4. God, man
5. Church, Grace

Page 162. A Test
1. Strength of will
2. Strength of mind
3. Strength of muscle
4. Strength of grace

Page 169. A Test

The correct answer to all the questions is *Yes*.

Page 171. The Law of Grace
1. Jesus, Source
2. fullness
3. Old, New
4. Paraclete
5. Holy Ghost, all
6. truth
7. New, Grace
8. Holy Ghost

Answers to the Tests: Book Four

Page 174. Baptism, Holy Eucharist, and Confirmation
1. Baptism
2. Grace
3. Holy Eucharist
4. Baptism, Holy Eucharist
5. Confirmation, soldiers
6. Confirmation
7. Christ, Church
8. all

Page 180. The Ceremonies of Confirmation
1. Bishop
2. Holy Ghost
3. extended, confirmed
4. God, confirmed, Spirit
5. Holy Ghost
6. wisdom, understanding, counsel, fortitude, knowledge, godliness, fear
7. chrism, Cross, Cross, chrism, forehead
8. chrism, Father, Son, Holy Ghost

Page 187. A Test

The correct groupings:
A Living Temple: 1, 2, 4, 7, 8, 10
A Temple of Stone: 3, 5, 6, 9

Page 190. A Test
1. The will
2. We love with the will.
3. God's Love
4. Wisdom
5. Charity

Page 192. A Test
1. The mind
2. We know and believe with the mind.
3. Mysteries of Faith
4. Understanding
5. Faith

Page 193. A Test
1. Hope
2. The power and might of God
3. The will
4. The dangers to his soul's salvation
5. Counsel

Page 194. A Test
1. The will
2. Work and suffer
3. Virtue of fortitude
4. Gift of fortitude
5. Father Isaac Jogues, S. J.

Page 196. A Test
1. The mind
2. The Light of God
3. Prudence
4. The Fiery Spirit of Knowledge
5. To see all sides of a question

Page 197. A Test
1. The will
2. Justice
3. As his Father
4. God and man
5. The Fiery Spirit of Piety

Page 198. A Test
1. The will
2. Temperance
3. His conscience
4. His own lowliness
5. The Fiery Spirit of Holy Fear

Answers to the Tests: Book Four

Page 201. A Test

The correct groupings are:

The deadly sin	The gift which gives the power to conquer the sin	The conquering quality in the gift
Pride	Holy Fear	A deep conviction of one's own lowliness
Envy	Gift of Piety	The desire to satisfy fully and lovingly the demands of justice
Anger	Gift of Knowledge	The light to see clearly the difference between right and wrong
Sloth	Gift of Fortitude	The desire, courage, and strength to undertake difficult things for God and carry them through
Covetousness	Gift of Counsel	The desire for eternal and heavenly riches
Gluttony	Gift of Understanding	The power to see the value of heavenly things
Lust	Gift of Wisdom	The enjoyment of the Master's Presence within His temple

Page 203. A Test

The correct choices:
1. he values the things of God above everything else.
2. his choice of vocation is based upon giving the greatest service to God.

Page 204. A Test

The correct choices:
1. she did a great kindness to Ann, although she knew that Ann had told a lie about her.
2. he gave his life to bring the Light of Grace to as many pagans as possible.

Page 206. A Test

The correct choices:
1. he felt so sorry to see God's Love ignored and sin committed by many people that he chose to be a priest.
2. when the Master came, he was willing to give up his own power and his own disciples.

Page 207. A Test

The correct choices:
1. he sacrificed all of his spending money to send it to the foreign missions.
2. she offered her life of work, prayer, and suffering to promote the interests of God's kingdom.

Page 209. A Test

The correct choices:
1. she used her spending money and influenced her friends to give their money so that she could bring food and clothing to a poor crippled child.
2. she gave all the wealth of her kingdom in charity and forgave big injuries.

Page 210. A Test

The correct choices:
1. he valued purity so much that he is called the Angelic Doctor.
2. no matter what she is doing, she always thinks of her Divine Lover and His right over the temple where He dwells.

Page 212. A Test

The correct choices:
1. he did the breakfast dishes for nine days in place of his sister, who wanted to go to Holy Mass every morning during a novena.
2. she used her influence to put an end to strife between kingdoms that were quarreling.

THE BALTIMORE CATECHISM NUMBER TWO

Where the Doctrinal Points of the Baltimore Catechism can be found in The Spiritual Way

Lesson 1: The End of Man

Catechism Question	Doctrinal Points	Where Taught BOOK	PAGES	TOPIC
1	God made the world.	I	1–7	1
2	God is the Creator of heaven and earth, etc.	I	1–7	1
3	Man is a creature composed of body and soul and made to the image and likeness of God.	I I II	8–10 26–40 1–15	1 2 5
4	This likeness is chiefly in the soul.	I II	38 9, 10, 14	2 5
5	The soul is like God because it is a spirit that will never die, and has understanding and free will.	I II III	26–29 16 6–7	2 5 10
6	God made me to know Him, to love Him, etc.	II II	22–39 52–55	6 7
7, 8	We must take more care of our soul than of our body.	II II	16–18 40–42	5 6
9	To save our souls we must worship God, etc.	II II	44–48 107	6 9
10	We shall know the things we are to believe from the Catholic Church, etc.	IV	1–38	15
11, 12	The Apostles' Creed	I I III IV	71 94 45–47 66–71	3 4 11 16

Lesson 2: God and His Perfections

13	God is a spirit infinitely perfect.	III	6–7	10
14	God had no beginning, etc.	III	7	10

The Spiritual Way: Manual

Catechism Question	Doctrinal Points	Where Taught		
		BOOK	PAGES	TOPIC
15	God is everywhere.	I	88, 91, 92 105	4
		Man.	33–34	
16	We do not see God because He is a pure spirit, etc.	III	6, 7, 17	10
17	God sees us and watches over us.	I	83–94	4
18	God knows all things, etc.	I	83–94	4
19	God can do all things, etc.	I	57–70	3
	Lesson 3: The Unity and Trinity of God			
20	God is all just, etc.	II	101	8
		III	7	10
		III	31	11
		IV	104	17
21	There is but one God.	III	11, 13, 14	10
23	In God there are three Divine Persons.	III	9, 10, 13	10
24	The Father is God, etc.	III	13–14	10
25	The Son is God, etc.	III	13–14	10
26	The Holy Ghost is God, etc.	III	13–14	10
27	By the Blessed Trinity, I mean, etc.	III	11, 21	10
28	The three Divine Persons are equal, etc.	III	10, 13	10
29	The three Divine Persons are one and the same God, etc.	III	11, 12, 13	10
30	We cannot fully understand how the three Divine Persons are one, etc.	III	3, 9	10
31	A mystery is a truth which we cannot fully understand.	III	2, 3, 4	10
	Lesson 4: Creation			
32	God created heaven and earth, etc.	I	4–7	1
33	God created heaven and earth from nothing, etc.	I	4–7	1

The Catechism

Catechism Question	Doctrinal Points	Where Taught		
		BOOK	PAGES	TOPIC
34	The chief creatures of God, etc.	I	10–11	1
35	Angels are pure spirits, etc.	I	10–11	1
		II	68	7
		III	6	10
36	The angels were also created to assist, etc.	I	11	1
		II	68	7
38	All the angels did not remain good, etc.	I	102	4

LESSON 5: OUR FIRST PARENTS AND THE FALL

39	The first man and woman were Adam and Eve.	II	88	8
40	Adam and Eve were innocent and holy, etc.	II	88–89	8
41	To try their obedience, etc.	II	84–85	8
42	The chief blessings intended for Adam, etc.	II	83–84	8
43	Adam and Eve did not remain faithful, etc.	II	87	8
44	Adam and Eve, on account of their sin, lost innocence and holiness, etc.	II	88–89	8
45	On account of the disobedience of our first parents, we all share, etc.	II	88–90	8
46	Our nature was corrupted by the sin of our first parents, etc.	II	90	8
47	The sin we inherit from our first parents is called original sin.	II	90–91	8
48	This sin is called original because, etc.	II	90	8
49	This corruption of our nature and other punishments remain, etc.	II	88–90	8
		II	109–112	9
50	The Blessed Virgin Mary, through the merits of her Divine Son, etc.	III	66–69	12

The Spiritual Way: Manual

Lesson 6: Sin and Its Kinds

Catechism Question	Doctrinal Points	Where Taught		
		BOOK	PAGES	TOPIC
51	Original sin is not the only kind of sin.	II	108–109	9
52	Actual sin	IV	54	16
53	There are two kinds of actual sin, etc.	II	108, 113, 114	9
54	Mortal sin is a grievous offence, etc.	II	108	9
55	This sin is called mortal because, etc.	II	109	9
56	To make a sin mortal, etc.	II	108–111	9
57	Venial sin is a slight offence, etc.	II	113–114	9
58	The effects of venial sin, etc.	II	113–116	9
59	The chief sources of sin are seven, etc.	IV	199–200	20

Lesson 7: The Incarnation and Redemption

60	God did not abandon man, etc.	III	31	11
61	Our Blessed Lord and Saviour Jesus Christ is the Redeemer, etc.	III	38–39	11
62	I believe that: Jesus Christ is the Son of God, etc.	III	33, 34, 36, 39	11
63	Jesus Christ is true God because, etc.	III	60, 62, 63	11
64	Jesus Christ is true man because, etc.	III	34, 60	11
		III	76	12
65	In Jesus Christ there are two natures, etc.	III	33, 38	11
		III	67	12
66	No, Jesus Christ is but one Divine Person.	III	13	10
		III	60–62	11
67	Jesus Christ was always God as He is the second Person of the Blessed Trinity, etc.	III	13	10
		III	41–43	11
		IV	4	15
68, 69	By the Incarnation, I mean, etc.	III	76–77	12

The Catechism

Catechism Question	Doctrinal Points	Where Taught		
		BOOK	PAGES	TOPIC
70	The Son of God was conceived and made man by the power of the Holy Ghost.	III	66	12
71	The Blessed Virgin Mary is truly the Mother of God, etc.	III III	34 67, 71, 79	11 12
72	The Son of God was promised as a Redeemer, etc.	III	31–33	11
73	They who lived before the Son of God became man could be saved, etc.	I III	58 39–40	3 11
74	The Son of God was conceived and made man on Annunciation Day, etc.	III	72, 76, 77	12
75	Christ was born on Christmas Day, etc.	III	79	12
76	Christ lived on earth about thirty-three years, etc.	III	34–36	11
77	Christ lived so long on earth to show us, etc.	III IV	35, 38 2	11 15

LESSON 8: OUR LORD'S PASSION AND ASCENSION

78, 79	Jesus Christ was crucified and died on Good Friday.	III	36, 50–52	11
80	We call that day "Good" because, etc.	III	36	11
81, 82	Christ died on Mount Calvary, etc.	III	36, 48	11
83, 84	Christ suffered and died for our sins.	III	38, 39, 41, 48	11
85, 86, 87	After Christ's death, His soul descended into hell.	III	39–40	11
88	While Christ's soul was in limbo, etc.	III	40	11
89	Christ rose from the dead on Easter Sunday, etc.	III	41–42	11

166 The Spiritual Way: Manual

Catechism Question	Doctrinal Points	Where Taught		
		BOOK	PAGES	TOPIC
90	Christ stayed on earth forty days, etc.	III	42	11
		IV	31	15
		IV	80-81	17
91	After forty days Christ ascended into heaven, etc.	III	42	11
		IV	32-33	15

LESSON 9: THE HOLY GHOST AND HIS DESCENT UPON THE APOSTLES

94	The Holy Ghost is the Third Person of the Holy Trinity.	III	13	10
96	The Holy Ghost is equal to the Father, etc.	III	13	10
97, 98, 99	The Holy Ghost came down upon the Apostles, etc.	III	20	10
		IV	31-33	15
		IV	163-166	20
100, 101	The Holy Ghost will abide with the Church forever, etc.	IV	38	15

LESSON 10: THE EFFECTS OF THE REDEMPTION

102	Chief effects of the Redemption	III	38, 39, 41	11
103	Sanctifying grace is that grace, etc.	I	31-37	2
104, 105	(*Sanctifying grace* is the underlying theme in all the Topics of *The Spiritual Way* series. This is particularly true in Book Four, which treats of the Sacraments. Pages are, therefore, given only for the first presentation of the subject of grace.)			
106	Divine virtues of Faith, Hope and Charity are, etc.	IV	188-193	20

Catechism Question	Doctrinal Points	Where Taught		
		BOOK	PAGES	TOPIC
107	Faith is a divine virtue, etc.	IV	191	20
108	Hope is a divine virtue, etc.	IV	192	20
109	Charity is a divine virtue, etc.	IV	189	20
110	Actual grace	Man.	66	
111	Grace is necessary to salvation, etc.	II	57–60	7
112	We can and often do resist, etc.	II	109	9

Lesson 11: The Church

114	The means instituted by Our Lord, etc.	IV	2, 7, 13, 28, 35, 38	15
		IV	46	16
116	Jesus Christ is the invisible Head of the Church.	IV	14, 19, 28	15
117	Our Holy Father, the Pope, is the vicar of Christ, etc.	IV	14	15
118	The Pope, the successor of St. Peter, etc.	IV	9, 14	15
119	The successors of the other Apostles are the bishops, etc.	IV	4, 7, 8	15
120	Christ founded the Church to teach, etc.	IV	2, 3, 4, 8, 10, 17, 28	15
		IV	41, 44, 46	16
121	He who knows the Church to be the true Church, etc.	IV	51	16

Lesson 12: The Attributes and Marks of the Church

122	By the authority of the Church, I mean, etc.	IV	4, 5, 8, 9, 14	15
123				
124	By the infallibility of the Church, I mean, etc.	IV	35–38	15
126	By the indefectibility of the Church, I mean, etc.	IV	8–9	15

The Spiritual Way: Manual

Catechism Question	Doctrinal Points	Where Taught		
		BOOK	PAGES	TOPIC
127	These attributes are found in their fullness in the Pope.	IV	37	15
128	The Church has four marks, etc.	IV	17–19	15
129	The Church is One, because, etc.	IV	17	15
130	The Church is Holy, etc.	IV	17	15
131	The Church is Catholic, or universal, etc.	IV	17	15
132	The Church is Apostolic, etc.	IV	17	15
133	These attributes and marks are, etc.	IV	18–19	15
134	The Church derives its undying life and infallible authority, etc.	IV	32, 38	15
135	The Church is made and kept One, etc.	IV	170–171	20

Lesson 13: The Sacraments in General

136	A Sacrament is an outward sign, etc.	IV	47	16
137	There are seven Sacraments, etc.	IV	44	16
138	The Sacraments have the power of giving grace, etc.	IV	44	16
139–143	Some of the Sacraments give sanctifying grace and others increase it in our souls.	IV	49	16
		IV	83	17
		IV	121	18
		IV	148, 151, 154	19
		IV	168	20
147	Sacraments always give grace, etc.	IV	44–45	16
		IV	82	17
148	The Sacraments that we can receive more than once, etc.	IV	82	18
		IV	121	18
		IV	146, 154	19
149	The Sacraments that we can receive but once, etc.	IV	152	19

Catechism Question	Doctrinal Points	Where Taught		
		BOOK	PAGES	TOPIC
150, 151	The character which these Sacraments imprint, etc.	IV	152	19

Lesson 14: Baptism

152	Baptism is a Sacrament, etc.	IV	51	16
153	Actual sins and all punishments are remitted, etc.	IV	51	16
154	Baptism is necessary to salvation, etc.	IV	51	16
155	The priest is the ordinary minister of Baptism, etc.	IV	55	16
156	Whoever baptizes should pour water on the head, etc.	IV	50–52	16
157	There are three kinds of Baptism, etc.	IV	53–54	16
158	Baptism of water, etc.	IV	53	16
159	Baptism of desire, etc.	IV	54	16
160	Baptism of blood, etc.	IV	53	16
161	Baptism of desire or of blood, etc.	IV	53–54	16
162	In Baptism we promise, etc.	IV	66	16
164	Godfathers and godmothers are given, etc.	IV	60–61	16
165	The obligation of a godfather and a godmother, etc.	IV	60–61	16

Lesson 15: Confirmation

166	Confirmation is a Sacrament, etc.	IV	168–171	20
167	The Bishop is the ordinary minister, etc.	IV	177	20
168	The Bishop extends his hands, etc.	IV	178	20
169	Holy chrism is a mixture of olive oil, etc.	IV	175–176	20
170	In anointing the person he confirms, etc.	IV	179	20

Catechism Question	Doctrinal Points	Where Taught		
		BOOK	PAGES	TOPIC
171	By anointing the forehead with chrism is meant, etc.	IV	181	20
172	The Bishop gives the person a slight blow on the cheek, etc.	IV	181	20
173	To receive Confirmation worthily, etc.	IV	177	20
174	Persons of an age to learn should know, etc.	IV	176–177	20

LESSON 16: THE GIFTS AND FRUITS OF THE HOLY GHOST

176	The effects of Confirmation, etc.	IV	174, 186	20
177	The gifts of the Holy Ghost, etc.	IV	188	20
178	The gift of Fear of the Lord, etc.	IV	198	20
179	The gift of Piety	IV	197	20
180	The gift of Knowledge	IV	195	20
181	The gift of Fortitude	IV	194	20
182	The gift of Counsel	IV	192	20
183	The gift of Understanding	IV	191	20
184	The gift of Wisdom	IV	189	20
185	The Beatitudes	IV	202–213	20
186	The fruits of the Holy Ghost	IV	214–222	20

LESSON 17: THE SACRAMENT OF PENANCE

187	Penance is a Sacrament, etc.	IV	81–82	17
188	The Sacrament of Penance remits sins, etc.	IV	81–82	17
189	The priest has the power of absolving sins, etc.	IV	80–81	17
190	The priests of the Church exercise the power of forgiving sins, etc.	IV	82	17
191	To receive the Sacrament of Penance worthily, etc.	IV	86–91	17

The Catechism

Catechism Question	Doctrinal Points	Where Taught		
		BOOK	PAGES	TOPIC
192–194	The examination of conscience, etc.	IV	87	17

Lesson 18: Contrition

195	Contrition, or sorrow for sin, is a hatred of sin, etc.	IV	76, 77, 82, 87, 92, 93	17
197	When I say that our sorrow should be interior, etc.	IV	92–93	17
199	Our sorrow should be universal.	IV	88, 89, 99, 100	17
200	Our sorrow should be sovereign.	IV	92	17
201	We should be sorry for our sins, etc.	IV	92	17
202, 203	Perfect contrition and imperfect contrition, etc.	IV	92	17
204	Imperfect contrition is that, etc.	IV	92	17
206	A firm purpose of sinning no more, etc.	IV	93	17
207	Near occasions of sin, etc.	IV	93	17

Lesson 19: Confession

208	Confession is the telling of our sins, etc.	IV	86–88	17
209	We are bound to confess all our mortal sins, etc.	IV	99–100	17
210–213	The chief qualities of a good Confession, etc.	IV	84, 85, 88, 99, 100	17
214	If we cannot remember the number of our sins, etc.	IV	88	17
215	If without our fault we forget, etc.	IV	99	17
216	It is a grievous offence wilfully to conceal, etc.	IV	100	17
217	He who has wilfully concealed a mortal sin in confession, etc.	IV	99–100	17

The Spiritual Way: Manual

Catechism Question	Doctrinal Points	Where Taught BOOK	PAGES	TOPIC
218	The priest gives us a penance, etc.	IV	89	17
219	The Sacrament of Penance remits the eternal punishment, etc.	IV	105	17
220	God requires a temporal punishment, etc.	IV	105–106	17
221	The chief means by which we satisfy God, etc.	IV	105–107, 109	17
222	The chief spiritual works of mercy are, etc.	I	76–77	3
		I	101	4
		II	66–67	7
		IV	62–63	16
		IV	109, 110, 115	17
		IV	204	20
223	The chief corporal works of mercy are, etc.	III	43	11
		IV	208–209, 211, 212, 213	20

Lesson 20: The Manner of Making a Good Confession

224	On entering the confessional, etc.	IV	88	17
225	The first things we should tell the priest, etc.	IV	88	17
226	After telling the time of our last confession, etc.	IV	88	17
227	When the confessor asks us questions, etc.	IV	89	17
228	After telling our sins we should listen, etc.	IV	89	17
229	We should end our Confession, etc.	IV	89	17
230	While the priest is giving us absolution, etc.	IV	89	17

The Catechism

Lesson 21: Indulgences

Catechism Question	Doctrinal Points	Where Taught		
		BOOK	PAGES	TOPIC
231	An indulgence is the remission, etc.	IV	112	17
232	An indulgence is not a pardon, etc.	IV	114	17
233	There are two kinds of indulgences.	IV	114–115	17
234	A plenary indulgence is full remission, etc.	IV	114	17
235	A partial indulgence is remission of a part, etc.	IV	114	17
236	The Church by means of indulgences, etc.	IV	108–111	17
237	To gain an indulgence we must be, etc.	IV	114	17

Lesson 22: The Holy Eucharist

238	The Holy Eucharist is the Sacrament, etc.	IV	121	18
239	Christ instituted the Holy Eucharist, etc.	III	122–123	14
		IV	119–120	18
240	When Our Lord instituted the Holy Eucharist, etc.	III	118	14
241	Our Lord instituted the Holy Eucharist by taking bread, etc.	III	122–123	14
242	When Our Lord said, "This is my body," etc.	III	123	14
244	After the substance of the bread and wine had been changed, etc.	III	123	14
246	Transubstantiation is, etc.	Man.	59	
247	The substance of the bread and wine was changed, etc.	III	123	14
		IV	137	18
248	This change of bread and wine, etc.	III	124	14
249	Christ gave His priests the power to change bread, etc.	III	124	14
		IV	120	18

The Spiritual Way: Manual

Catechism Question	Doctrinal Points	Where Taught		
		BOOK	PAGES	TOPIC
250	The priests exercise this power, etc.	III	126	14
		IV	128	18

Lesson 23: The Ends for Which the Holy Eucharist Was Instituted

251	Christ instituted the Holy Eucharist, etc.	III	126–127	14
		IV	121, 123, 126, 127	18
252	We are united to Jesus Christ in the Holy Eucharist, etc.	IV	121, 127	18
253	Holy Communion is the receiving, etc.	III	136	14
254	To make a good Communion it is necessary, etc.	IV	138	18
255	He who receives Communion in mortal sin, etc.	IV	83–84	17
		IV	135–138	18
256	To receive plentifully the graces, etc.	IV	135–138	18
257	The fast necessary for Holy Communion, etc.	IV	138	18
258	Anyone in danger of death, etc.	IV	156	19
259	We are bound to receive Holy Communion, etc.	III	20	10
		IV	22–23	15
260	It is well to receive Holy Communion often.	IV	140–141	18
261	After Holy Communion we should spend some time, etc.	IV	139	18

Lesson 24: The Sacrifice of the Mass

262	The bread and wine are changed into the Body and Blood of Christ, etc.	III	132	14

The Catechism

Catechism Question	Doctrinal Points	Where Taught		
		BOOK	PAGES	TOPIC
263	The Mass is the unbloody Sacrifice of the Body and Blood of Christ.	III IV	126 120	14 18
264	A sacrifice is the offering of an object by a priest, etc.	III III IV	97 124-125 150	13 14 19
265	The Mass is the same Sacrifice as that of the Cross.	III	126	14
266	The Mass is the same Sacrifice as that of the Cross because, etc.	III	124, 125, 126	14
267	The ends for which the Sacrifice of the Cross was offered, etc.	III	146, 150, 151	14
268	Yes, the manner in which the Sacrifice is offered is different, etc.	III IV	124, 125, 126 120	14 18
269	We should assist at Mass with great interior recollection, etc.	III	133, 138	14
270	The best manner of hearing Mass is to offer, etc.	III	133, 137, 138, 150	14

Lesson 25: Extreme Unction and Holy Orders

271	Extreme Unction is the Sacrament, etc.	IV	154	19
272	We should receive Extreme Unction when, etc.	IV	154, 156	19
273	We should not wait until, etc.	IV	156	19
274	The effects of Extreme Unction are, etc.	IV	154-155	19
275	By the remains of sin, I mean, etc.	II	113, 114, 116	9
276	We should receive the Sacrament of Extreme Unction, etc.	IV	156	19
277	The priest is the minister of the Sacrament, etc.	IV	156	19

Catechism Question	Doctrinal Points	Where Taught		
		BOOK	PAGES	TOPIC
278	Holy Orders is a Sacrament by which, etc.	IV	151	19
279	To receive Holy Orders worthily, it is necessary, etc.	IV	151, 153	19
280	Christians should look upon priests as messengers of God, etc.	IV	152	19
281	Bishops can confer the Sacrament of Holy Orders.	IV	151	19

Lesson 26: Matrimony

282	The Sacrament of Matrimony is a Sacrament, etc.	IV	146	19
283	Christ raised marriage to the dignity of a Sacrament, etc.	IV	147	19
284	Christian marriage cannot be dissolved, etc.	IV	147	19
285	The effects of the Sacrament of Matrimony are, etc.	IV	148	19
286	To receive the Sacrament of Matrimony worthily, etc.	IV	147	19
287	The Church alone has the right to make laws concerning, etc.	IV / IV	23 / 147	15 / 19
288	The Church does forbid the marriage of Catholics, etc.	IV	23	15
291	Christians should prepare for a holy and happy marriage, etc.	IV	147–149	19

Lesson 27: Sacramentals

292	A sacramental is anything set apart by the Church, etc.	IV	159	19
293	The difference between the Sacraments and sacramentals is, etc.	IV / IV	44 / 159	16 / 19

Catechism Question	Doctrinal Points	Where Taught		
		BOOK	PAGES	TOPIC
294	Chief sacramental used, etc.	IV	159	19
295	We make the Sign of the Cross, etc.	III	15	10
296	We make the Sign of the Cross to show, etc.	III	15–16	10
297	The Sign of the Cross is a profession of faith, etc.	III	15	10
299	The Sign of the Cross reminds us that the Son of God suffered death on the Cross.	Man.	46	
300	Another sacramental is holy water, etc.	III	16	10
		IV	159	19
302	Other sacramentals are blessed candles, etc.	IV	159	19

Lesson 28: Prayer

303	There is another means of obtaining God's grace, etc.	I	76–77	3
304	Prayer is the lifting up of our minds, etc.	III	17–18	10
305	Prayer is necessary to salvation, etc.	II	107	9
306	We should pray particularly on Sundays, etc.	I	98, 104	4
		II	28, 47	6
		II	74	7
307	We should pray: first with attention, etc.	I	72	3
		I	106–107	4
		II	27, 28, 36	6
		III	16–18	10
308	The prayers most recommended to us are The Lord's Prayer, etc.	I	71–72	3
		II	44–47	6
		III	46–47	11
		III	81–82	12
		IV	66–69	16
		IV	84, 92	17

Catechism Question	Doctrinal Points	Where Taught		
		BOOK	PAGES	TOPIC
309	Prayers said with wilful distractions, etc.	III	17–18	10

Lesson 29: The Commandments of God

310	It is not enough to belong to the Church to be saved, etc.	II IV	35 19	6 15
311	Commandments which contain the whole law of God, etc.	II	70–71	7
312	These two Commandments of the love of God, etc.	IV	95, 98	17
313	The Commandments of God are these ten, etc.	II	125	9
314	God Himself gave the ten Commandments, etc.	II	70	7

Lesson 30: The First Commandment

315	The first Commandment is, etc.	II	72	7
316	The first Commandment helps us to keep, etc.	II IV	70–72 95	7 17
317	We adore God by faith, hope, etc.	II	71–72	7
318	The first Commandment may be broken, etc.	II IV	71–72 96	7 17
321	A person sins against faith; first, etc.	II II IV	57, 78 124 183	7 9 20
323	Heretics and infidels	Man.	45	
324	They who neglect to profess their belief, etc.	IV	19	15
325	They who fail to profess faith in the true Church, etc.	IV IV	19 183	15 20

The Catechism

Catechism Question	Doctrinal Points	Where Taught		
		BOOK	PAGES	TOPIC
326	We are obliged to make open profession, etc.	IV	183	20
327–329	Presumption	Man.	45	
330	We sin against the love of God, etc.	II	31–32	6
		II	72	7
		II	109–111	9
		IV	95–99	17

Lesson 31: The First Commandment — The Honor and Invocation of Saints

331	The first Commandment does not forbid the honoring of saints, etc.	II	68	7
332		III	23	10
		III	58–59	11
		IV	167	20
333	By praying to the saints, we mean, etc.	II	67	7
334	We know that the saints hear us, etc.	II	68	7
335	We believe that the saints will help, etc.	II	65–66	7
336	The saints and we are members, etc.	II	65–66	7
337	The communion of the members of the Church, etc.	II	66	7
338	The Communion of Saints means the union, etc.	II	65–66	7
339	The following benefits are derived from, etc.	II	66–68	7
340	The first Commandment does not forbid, etc.	III	141	14
341, 343	The first Commandment does forbid the making of images, etc.	Man.	46	

Catechism Question	Doctrinal Points	Where Taught		
		BOOK	PAGES	TOPIC
342	It is right to show respect to the pictures, etc.	III IV	48–49 159	11 19
344	We pray before the crucifix, etc.	III IV	48–49 159	11 19

LESSON 32: THE SECOND AND THIRD COMMANDMENTS

345	The second Commandment is, etc.	II	73	7
346	We are commanded by the second Commandment, etc.	II	73	7
347	An oath is the calling upon God to witness the truth, etc.	II	73	7
348, 349	We may take an oath when it is ordered by lawful authority.	Man.	46	
350	A vow is a deliberate promise, etc.	II	73	7
351	It is a sin not to fulfill our vows, etc.	Man.	47	
352	The second Commandment forbids all false oaths, etc.	II	73	7
353	The third Commandment is, etc.	II	75	7
354	By the third Commandment, etc.	II	74–75	7
355	We are to worship God on Sundays, etc.	II	74–75	7
358	The third Commandment forbids, etc.	II	75	7

LESSON 33: THE FOURTH, FIFTH, AND SIXTH COMMANDMENTS

361	The fourth Commandment is, etc.	II	76	7
362	We are commanded by the fourth Commandment, etc.	II	76	7
363	We are also bound to honor and obey, etc.	I IV	78, 79 98	3 17
365	The fourth Commandment forbids all disobedience, etc.	II	76	7

The Catechism 181

Catechism Question	Doctrinal Points	Where Taught		
		BOOK	PAGES	TOPIC
366	The fifth Commandment is, etc.	II	77	7
367	We are commanded by the fifth Commandment, etc.	II	77	7
368	The fifth Commandment forbids, etc.	II	77	7
369	The sixth Commandment is, etc.	II	96	8
370	We are commanded by the sixth Commandment, etc.	II	98–101	8
371	The sixth Commandment forbids, etc.	II	96–98	8
372	The sixth Commandment forbids the reading, etc.	II	98	8

Lesson 34: The Seventh, Eighth, Ninth, and Tenth Commandments

373	The seventh Commandment is, etc.	II	120	9
374	By the seventh Commandment we are commanded, etc.	II	120	9
375	The seventh Commandment forbids, etc.	II	120	9
376	We are bound to restore ill-gotten goods, etc.	II	120	9
377	We are bound to repair the damage, etc.	II	120	9
378	The eighth Commandment is, etc.	II	121	9
379	We are commanded by the eighth Commandment, etc.	II	121	9
380	The eighth Commandment forbids, etc.	II	121	9
382	The ninth Commandment is, etc.	II	122	9
383	We are commanded by the ninth Commandment, etc.	II	122	9
384	The ninth Commandment forbids, etc.	II	97–98	9
		II	122	9
385	Impure thoughts and desires are, etc.	II	122	9

The Spiritual Way: Manual

Catechism Question	Doctrinal Points	Where Taught		
		BOOK	PAGES	TOPIC
386	The tenth Commandment is, etc.	II	123	9
387	By the tenth Commandment we are commanded, etc.	II	123	9
388	The tenth Commandment forbids, etc.	II	123	9

Lesson 35: The First and Second Commandments of the Church

389	The chief Commandments of the Church are six, etc.	IV	19	15
390	It is a mortal sin not to hear Mass, etc.	IV	19–20	15
391	Holy days were instituted, etc.	III	63	11
		III	84	12
		IV	20–21	15
392	We should keep the holy days of obligation, etc.	IV	20	15
393	By fast days I mean days, etc.	IV	22	15
394	By days of abstinence, etc.	IV	22	15
395	The Church commands us to fast and abstain, etc.	IV	22	15
		IV	108	17
396	The Church commands us to abstain, etc.	IV	22	15

Lesson 36: The Third, Fourth, Fifth, and Sixth Commandments of the Church

397	By the command of confessing, etc.	IV	22	15
398	We should confess frequently, etc.	IV	22	15
400	He who neglects to receive Communion, etc.	III	20	10
		IV	19	15
401	Easter time is, in this country, etc.	III	20	10
402	We are obliged to contribute to the support of pastors, etc.	IV	22–23	15

Catechism Question	Doctrinal Points	Where Taught		
		BOOK	PAGES	TOPIC
404, 405	The meaning of the precept not to solemnize marriage, etc.	IV	23	15
406, 407	A nuptial Mass, etc.	III	145	14

Lesson 37: The Last Judgment, Resurrection, Hell, Purgatory, and Heaven

408	Christ will judge us immediately, etc.	II	53, 57, 61	7
409	The Particular Judgment	Man.	109	
410	The General Judgment	Man.	54	
411	Christ judges men immediately to reward, etc.	II	53, 57, 61	7
412	The rewards or punishments appointed, etc.	II	53, 57, 61	7
413	Hell is a state to which the wicked are condemned, etc.	II	57–58	7
414	Purgatory is a state, etc.	II	61–62	7
		II	115	9
415	The faithful on earth can help the souls in purgatory, etc.	II	67	7
		IV	115	17
416	There is need of a General Judgment, etc.	III	42–43	11
		IV	105	17
417	Our bodies will share in the reward, etc.	III	42–43	11
		IV	69	16
418	The bodies of the just will rise, etc.	IV	68	16
419	The bodies of the damned will also rise, etc.	III	42–43	11
		IV	68	16
420	Heaven is the state of everlasting life, etc.	II	54	7
421	What doth it profit a man, etc.	Man.	55	

www.ingramcontent.com/pod-product-compliance
Lightning Source LLC
Chambersburg PA
CBHW070850050426
42453CB00012B/2114